LEAR
PENCIL SHADING
Nature & Still Life

by:
DILIP KADAM
BABU UDUPI

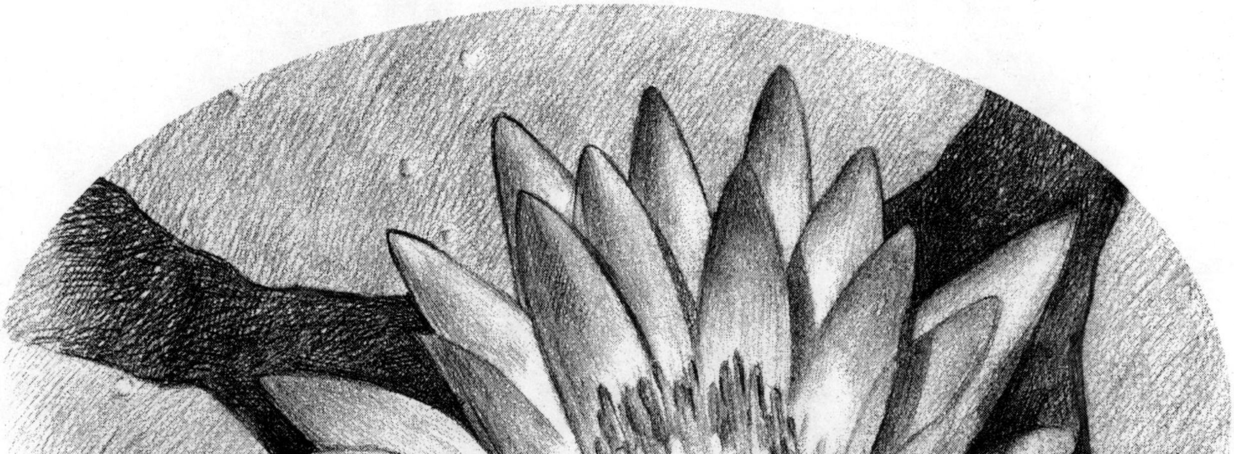

MANOJ PUBLICATIONS

Publishers :
Manoj Publications
761, Main Road, Burari
Delhi 110084
Phone : 27611116, 27611349
Fax : 27611546
Mobile : 9868112194
Website : www.manojpublications.com
E-mail : info@manojpublications.com

Showroom :
Manoj Publications
1583-84, Dariba Kalan
Chandni Chowk
Delhi 110006
Ph.: 23262174, 23268216
(M) 9818753569

Printers :
Jai Maya Offset
Delhi 110095

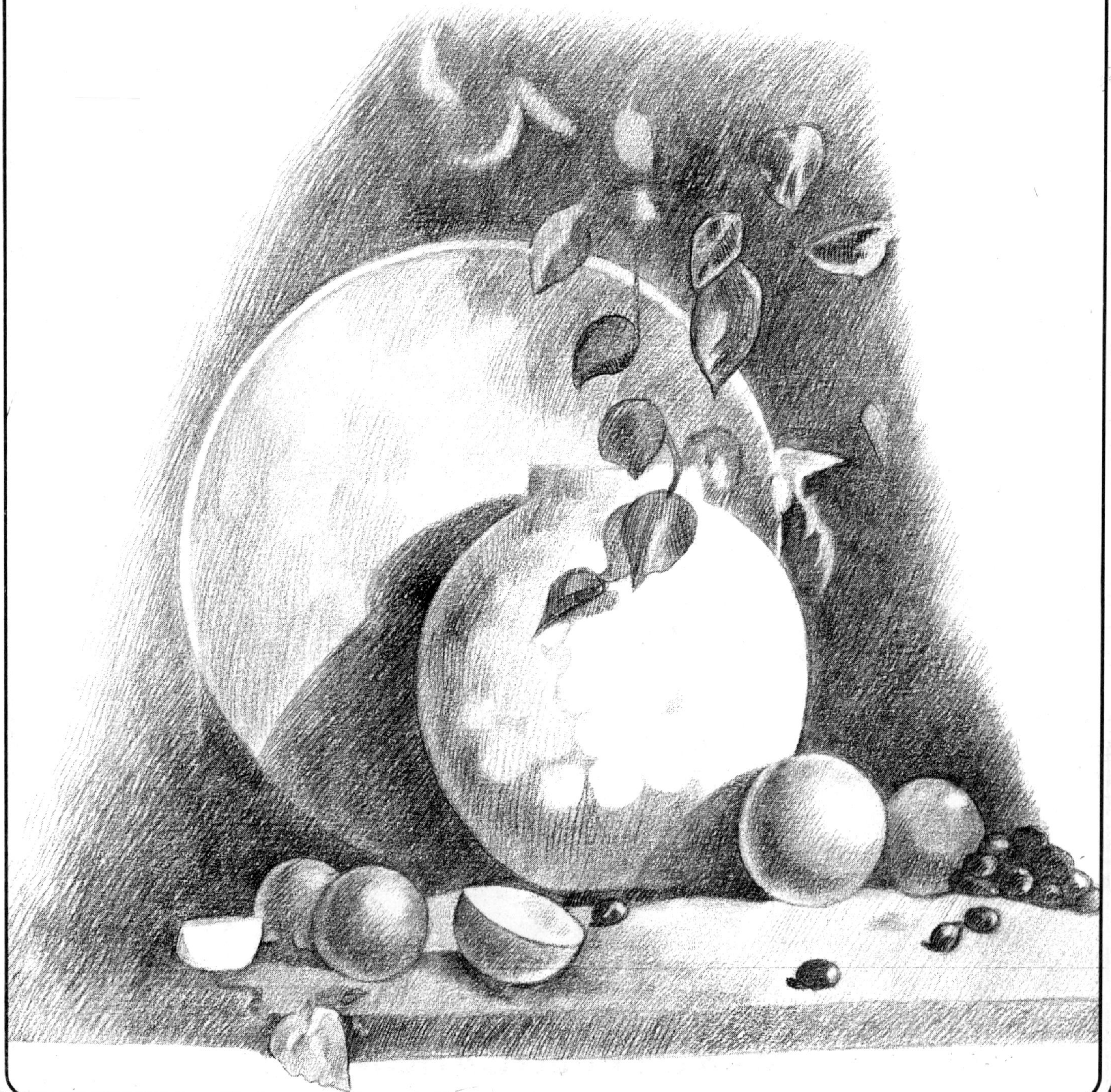

Dear Children,

Drawing is not only a wonderful art form in itself, but it is also an excellent exercise for other forms of art.

There are a variety of different drawing tools available today and what you choose to work with is based on your own preference. You have to work with a number of different things before you find the tools that fit your style of drawing.

Don't go out and spend tons of money on your drawing supplies in the beginning. You can really get started with a beginner pencil set and some news print paper. When you become more experienced, you can then venture out and spend money on better supplies.

It is important to remember the following points before you start drawing :

1. As you start shading the drawing, your hand tends to get dirty with lead powder. This has to be avoided, as it might spoil your drawing. You can do this by working downwards from the top to the bottom of the page whenever possible, or better still, you could make it a habit to place a clean sheet of paper under your hand while working.
2. Don't hurry while you draw. It will result in an untidy picture. Work patiently and complete the drawing step-by-step. You will need about 2-3 hours to complete a drawing study. Speed will come through practice.
3. Don't be disappointed if you are not happy with the shading in a certain part. Improve upon it with the help of an eraser or rub out that part totally and start anew.
4. After you finish shading, compare your drawing with the original one, it is important that the drawing reflects the personality of the subject. Pay special attention to this aspect and try to achieve the 'look' of the original.

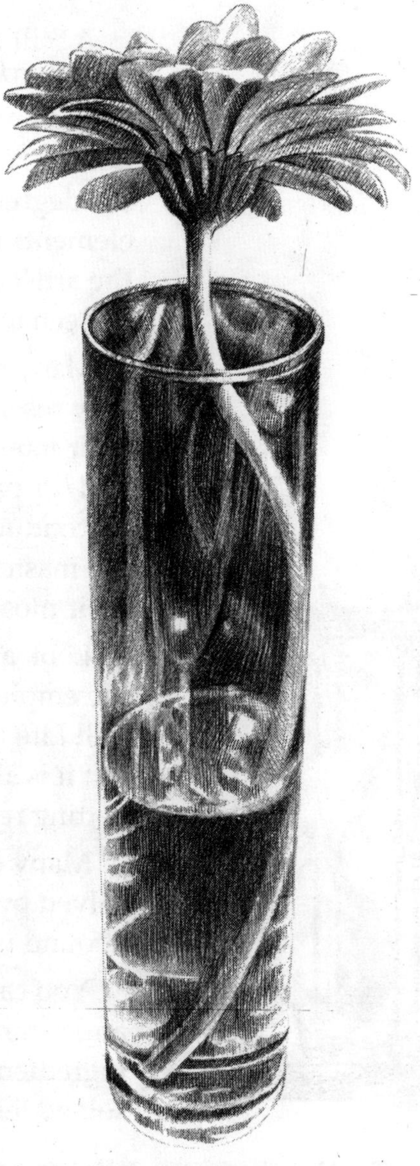

Avoid looking at your drawing too often. Make sure you are constantly focusing on the subject and only glancing at your drawing. By doing so, you won't constantly judge your drawing, or think something is wrong or out of place. Focus on the subject and draw what you see.

Never throw any of your drawings. Keep a neat portfolio of everything you draw. This is an excellent way to see your progress over time.

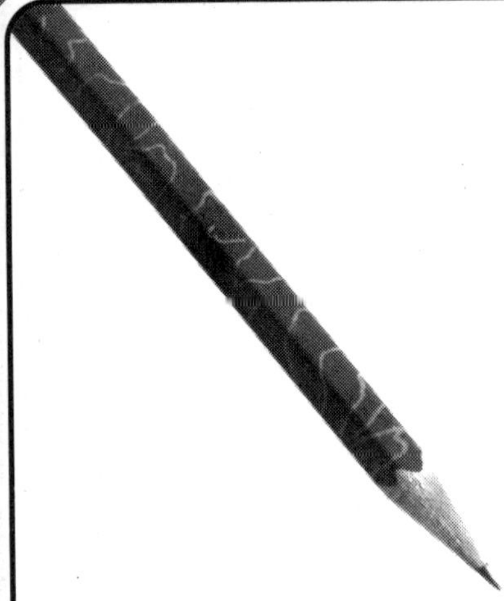

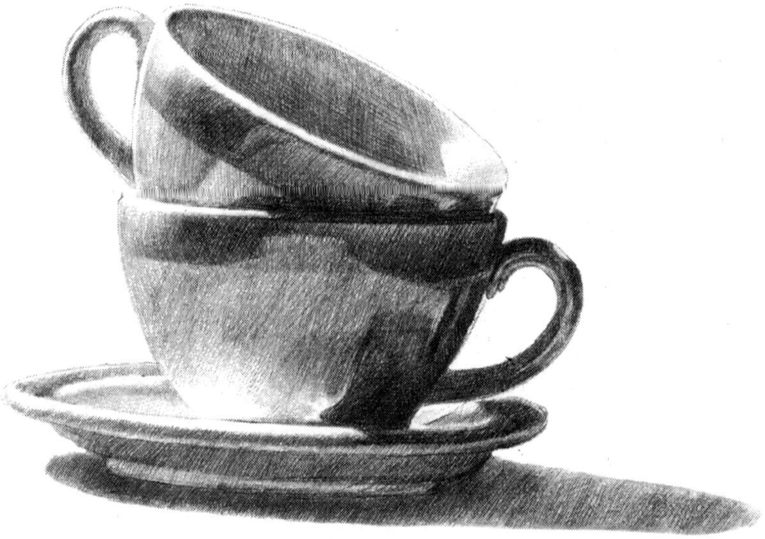

INTRODUCTION

A Still Life painting or photograph is the study of inanimate objects. These objects are typically those of everyday use and include plants, fruits, vegetables, dishes, soup cans and more. But, perhaps even more importantly, a key feature of still life art work is the degree of control that the artist can exercise over the work. The elements that make up a Still Life can be arranged or composed by the artist at will; the lighting can be redirected. Still Life painting can be seen to be a relatively pure, even abstract, form of art.

Many students find Still Life painting dull, probably because they resent the discipline entailed and are unable to sustain their interest. And there are art educators who claim that drawing and/or painting Still Life is just a mechanical exercise that cannot be conducive to expressive (and truly artistic) art. But if you study the masters, both classic and modern, you will notice that many of their most important works are still life paintings.

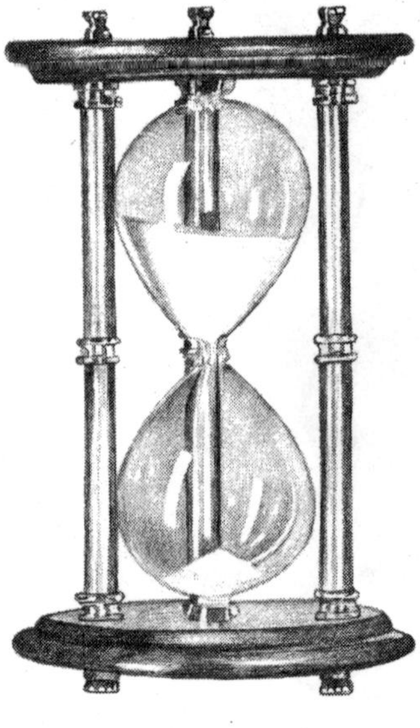

Look at masterpieces of portraiture in which Still Life accessories are employed, and see how important they are to the painting. Still Life painting is a complete and fascinating subject in itself, but it is also an excellent exercise for the beginner students who are getting ready to start painting outdoors.

Many of the problems that arise when painting landscapes can be solved by Still Life practice. Flowers, fruits, and vegetables are abound with both obvious and subtle colour.

You can create your own compositions, lighting effects, and arrangements. The important thing is that all these vital ingredients of successful painting can be studied and solved leisurely.

PENCILS/TOOLS

The pencil is the most familiar drawing tool and can be used in various exciting and expressive ways. Pencil of the 'H & B system' (hard & soft graphite) can be used to draw broad, soft & fine lines, by sharpening them accordingly. Other types of pencils include mechanical lead holder pencils or clutch pencils designed to be used with inter-changeable hard & soft leads.
Carpenter pencils have a flat rectangular lead allowing broad, grainy marks. Graphite sticks produce strong dark marks.

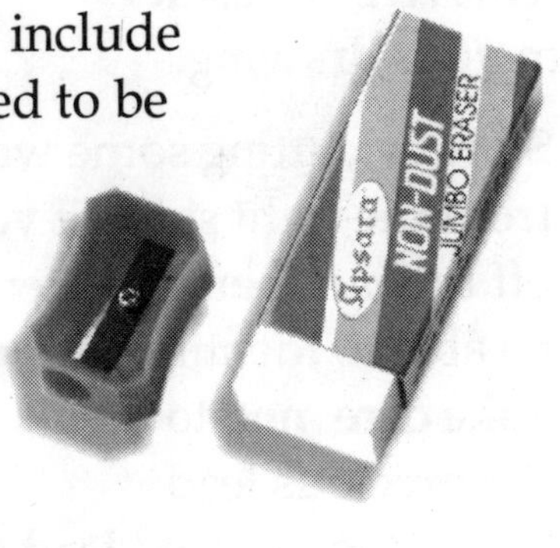

H, HB, the harder grades of lead produce fine light lines. 2B & 4B are popularly used for shading.

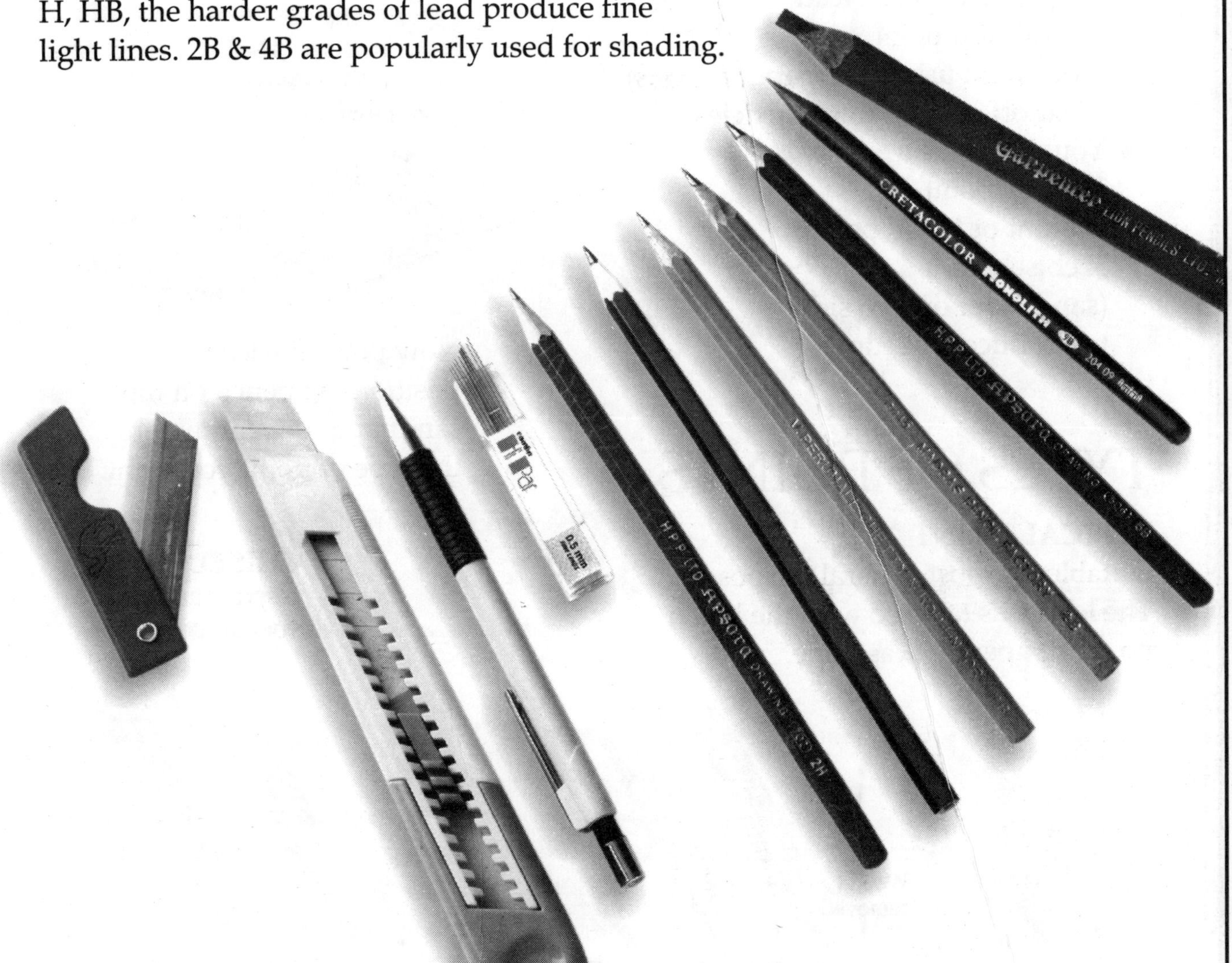

SHARPENING THE PENCIL

You must prepare your pencils
to achieve best results
from your drawing.

- Start by cutting some wood from the right side (if you whittle off the numbers or letters you won't be able to identify your pencil!). Take care not to break off the precious lead.
- Shape the exposed lead to a desired point (you could use a sandpaper for this).
- Clear off any graphite particles.
- You can make a
  1. sharp point
  2. blunt or broad point
  3. chisel point
  (sandpaper on two sides to produce thin edge)

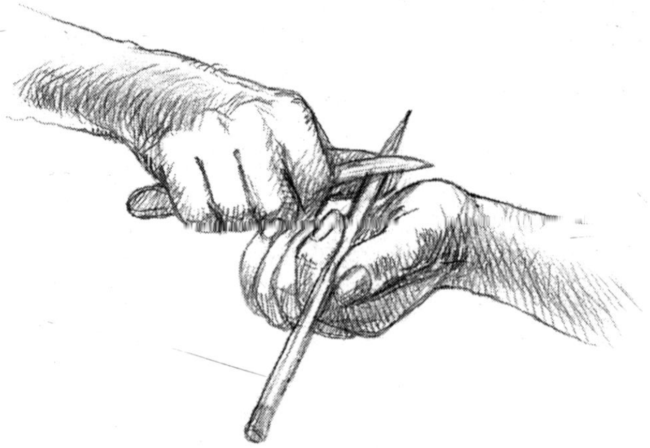

Start to sharpen the pencil by removing the wood.
Use a sharp knife or cutter and hold it naturally.

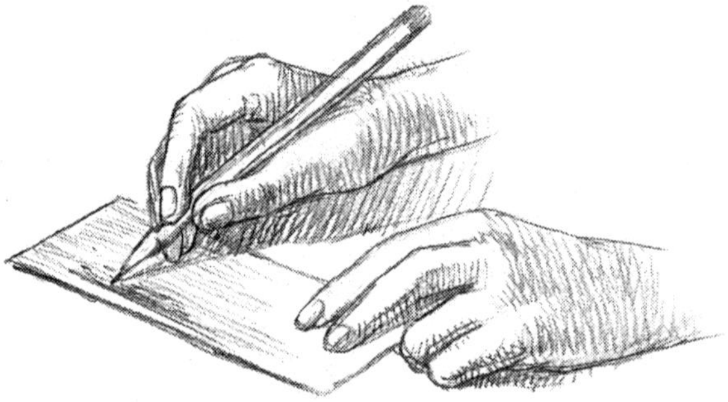

Now point the lead.
Position the pencil on the sandpaper depending on the type of point you want.

TYPES OF POINTS

TYPICAL POINT
Suitable for most general purposes.
The lead was tapered with the knife;
no sandpapering was done.

CHISEL POINT
Used mainly for
special purposes.

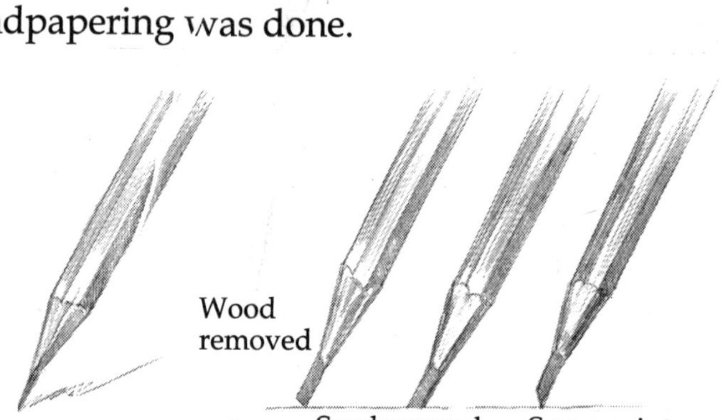

Sandpapered for broad lines

Same point inverted for fine lines

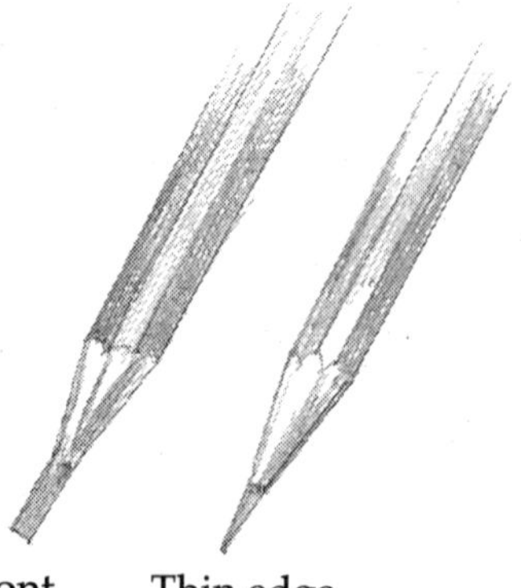

Front

Thin edge

HOLDING THE PENCIL

Holding the pencil correctly would depend on the position of your paper and the strokes you wish to achieve. The drawings alongside will amplify this.

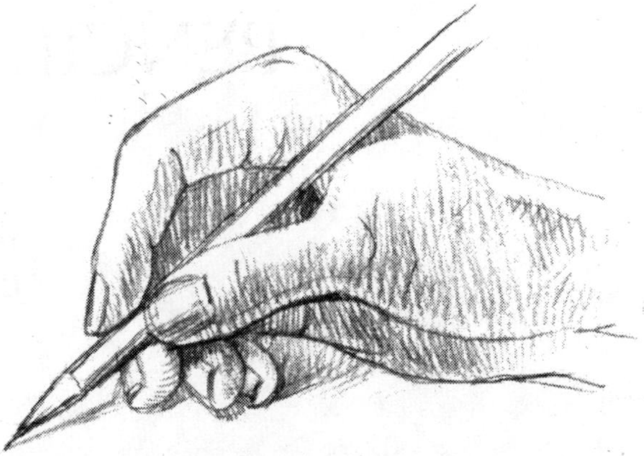

TYPICAL POSITION (variable)

For typical work most artists hold the pencil as if they were writing, with hand resting lightly on the table.

Notice the various positions used for holding the pencil. Vary the position to create the particular stroke you need for a given subject or effect.

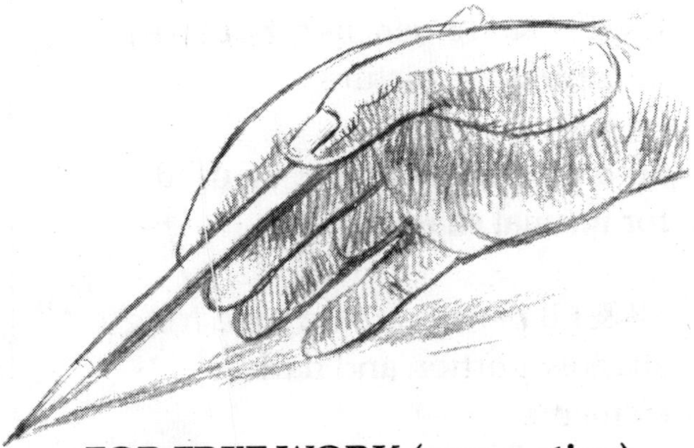

FOR FREE WORK (arm motion)

For longer strokes – the ones that are quick and dashing – hold the pencil well back from the point and swing the entire forearm and freely from elbow with a minimum of wrist and finger movement.

For most shaded work the quality of line and tone desired will determine your hand position, which may change frequently. Occasionally, you may want to keep the pencil almost vertical. This position sometimes proves useful when you want to build up tone very carefully with a sharp point.

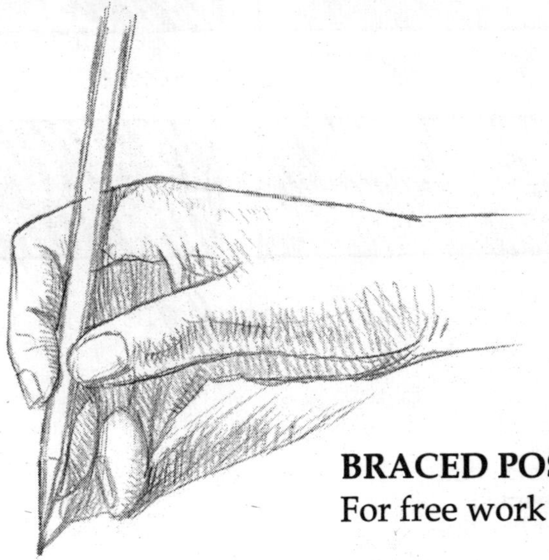

BRACED POSITION (for detail work)
For free work (arm motion)

PENCIL SHADING

This rendering requires normal uniform pressure.

These are done with uneven pressure to get proper type of tonal values, as and where required.

The pencil should be handled in specific ways to create effective light and shade, tonal value, texture of various kinds of objects and natural forms.

Use 2H & HB pencils for outlines or tracing the picture.

2B & 4B pencils should be used for normal shading.

4B & 6B pencils are for rendering shadow portion and dark elements.

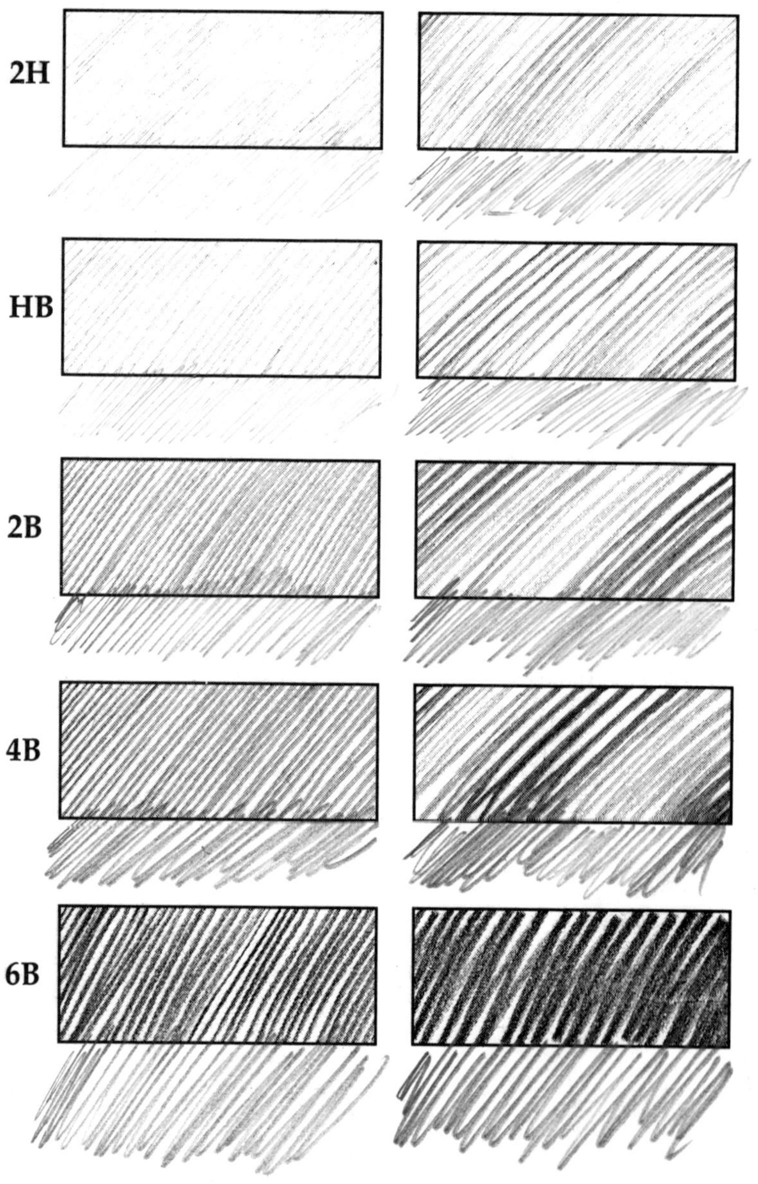

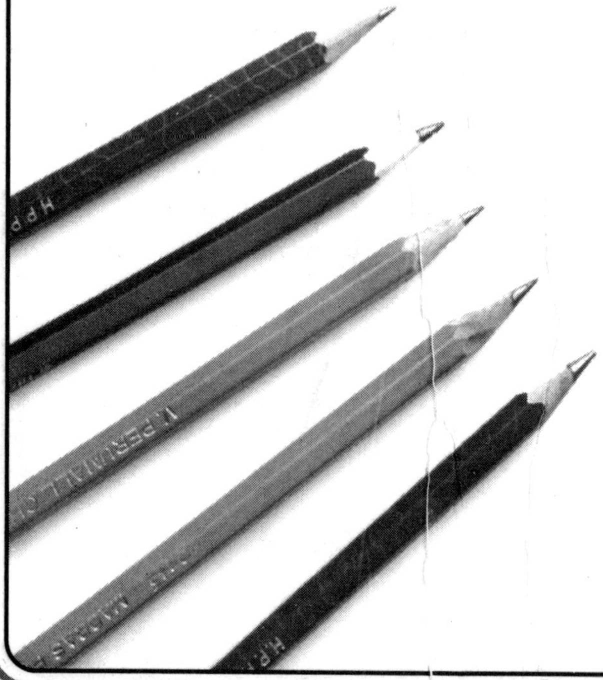

MODELLING LINES

There are subtleties of form which cannot be rendered with a single contour line. To convey these complexities of form, texture, and material, we can use several types of modelling lines, like hatching, scribbling, cross hatching, multi-directional lines etc. with the purpose to create required tonal values, network of random, multi-directional lines.

This is done with normal hatching (series of closely spaced parallel lines) with little pressure, mostly used in lighter portion.
(For details see page no. 3)

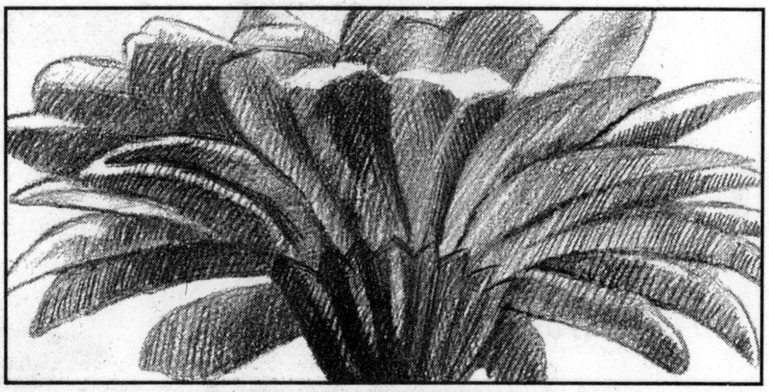

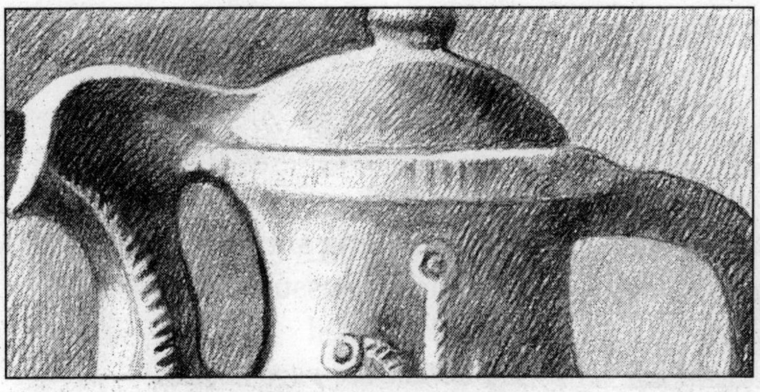

This one is cross hatching (layering two sets of hatched lines) normally used for dark tones.
(For details see page no. 28)

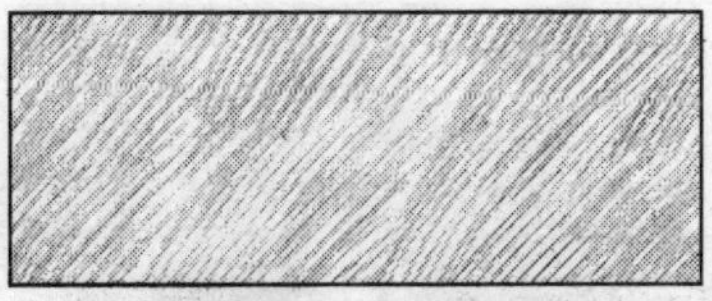

According to light & shade use uneven hatching.
(For details see page no. 20)

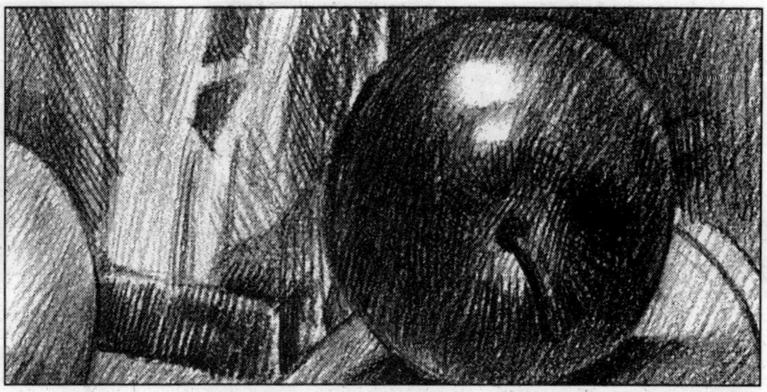

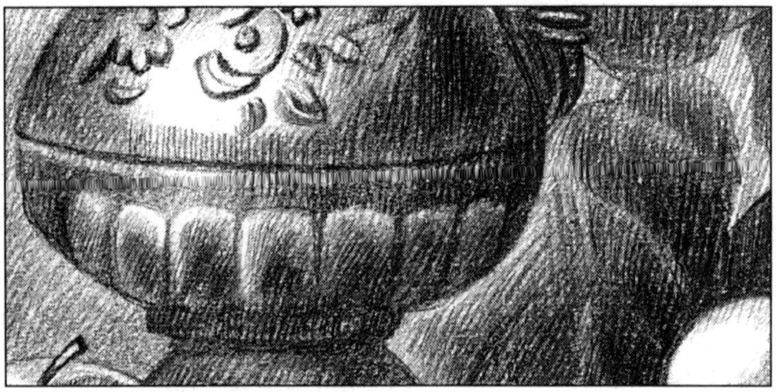

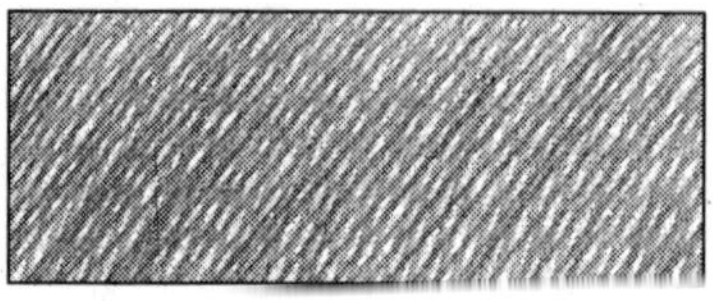

To get dark tonal values, first apply even strokes with hatching style, then smudge with finger, clean cloth or paper stump. After smudging, render with dark cross hatching strokes.
(For details see page no. 30)

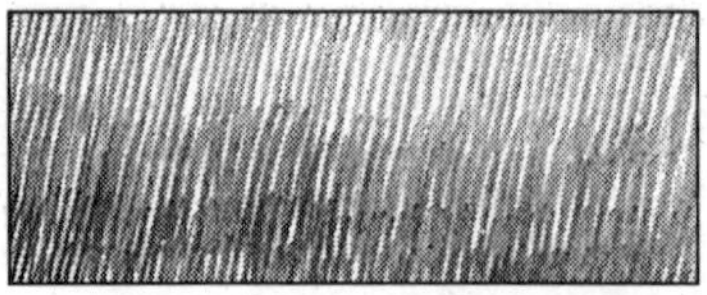

To get dark line tone, hatching should be done according to the form.
(For details see page no. 4)

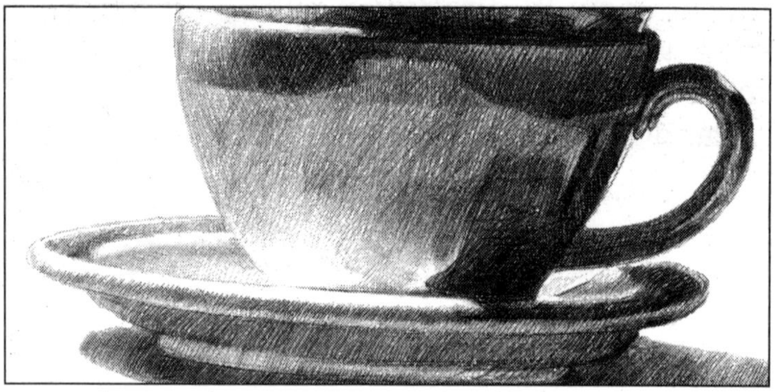

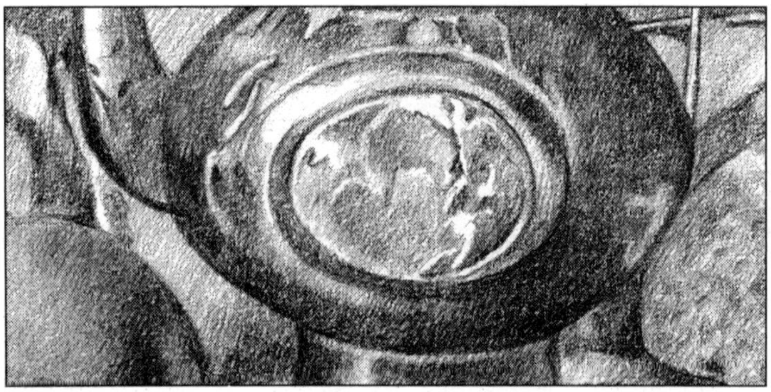

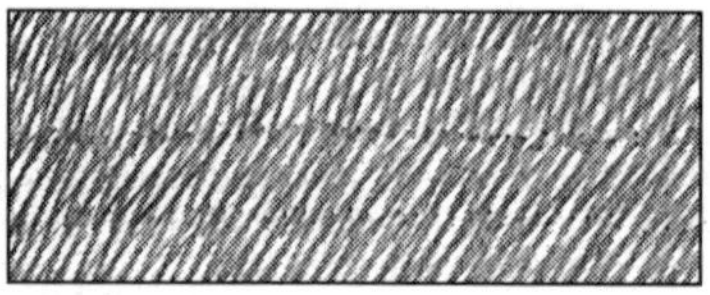

To get darker tone, cross hatching should be done with more pressure using 4B pencil.
(For details see page no. 16)

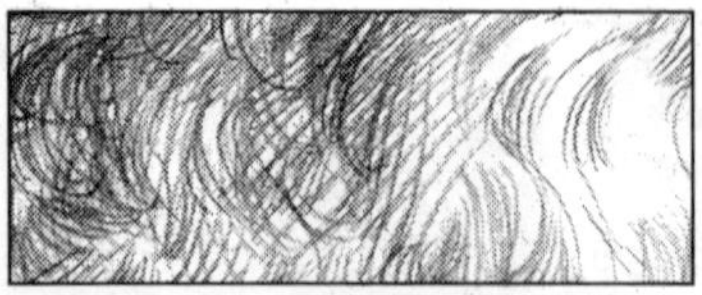

According to light & shade and shape of the object, to get rhythm of curved lines with even and uneven pressure, use soft pencil (2B/4B).
(For details see page no. 14)

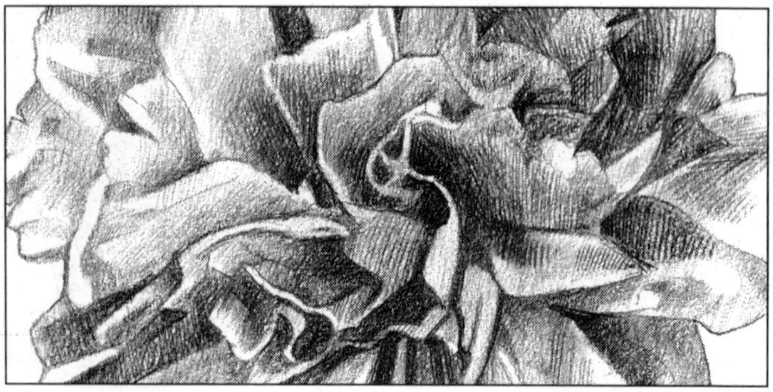

LIGHT & SHADE

Drawing done with light & dark shade help to create volume to any form. Various tonal values can be achieved by :

1. varying the pressure on the pencil
2. varying the grade of the pencil
3. repetition and over working

The drawings along side amplify this.

1. HIGHLIGHT
2. LIGHT TONE
3. SHADOW
4. REFLECTED LIGHT
5. CAST SHADOW

Good drawing begins with a search for simple basic forms. With the basic forms established, we can then build the surface forms. Then, since only light can define form, we must study carefully what the light does as it travels across the surfaces, noting the areas of light halftone and shadow. As the form turns away from the light it produces halftone and shadow. The lightness or darkness of the halftone is the result of angle of the plain in relation to the direction of the light. Shadows occur only when the light cannot reach the plane.

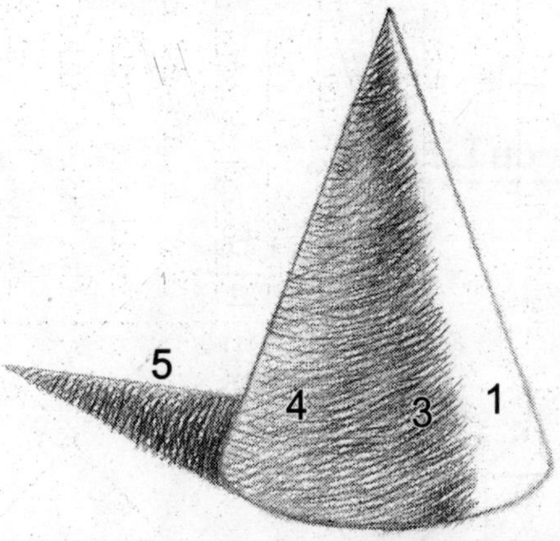

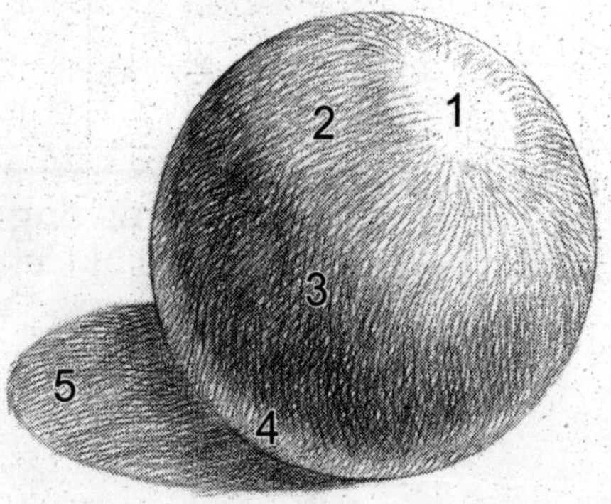

Think of the values as occurring in bands.

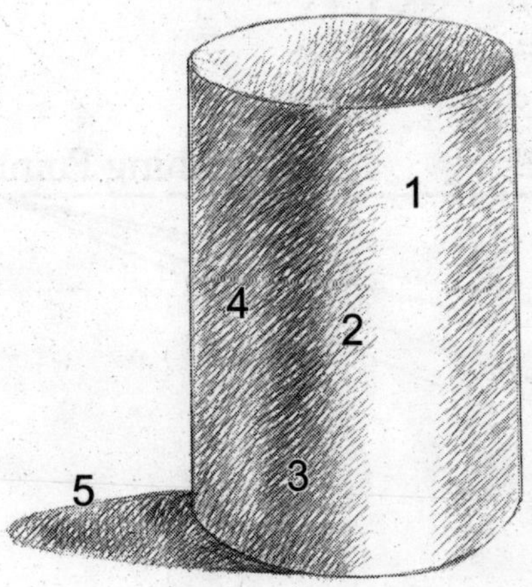

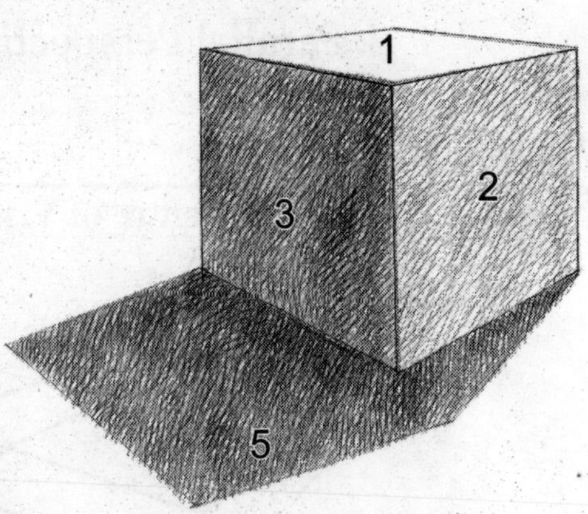

Note the band of the darker shadow that appears between the halftone of light and the reflected light within the shadow. The cast shadow on the ground plane start from this band.

PERSPECTIVE

Most of the stills life are viewed close up, you still need an understanding of basic perspective in order to draw objects such as cups, bowls, boxes, tables, and jars convincingly. Perspective is dependent on your view point. There are two basic types of perspectives Parallel and Oblique, (diagrams A and B), and both are easy to master once you identify the horizon line your centre of vision and the vanishing point. The horizon line is always at eye level and is found by looking straight ahead. Your centre of vision lies on the horizon line, the middle of the whatever direction your are looking, the vanishing point is the point on the horizon line at which all parallel lines that recede into the distance appear to converge. (Imagine standing in the middle of the road). With parallel perspective the vanishing point will also be your centre of vision whereas with an oblique perspective their will be two vanishing points—one on either side of your centre of vision

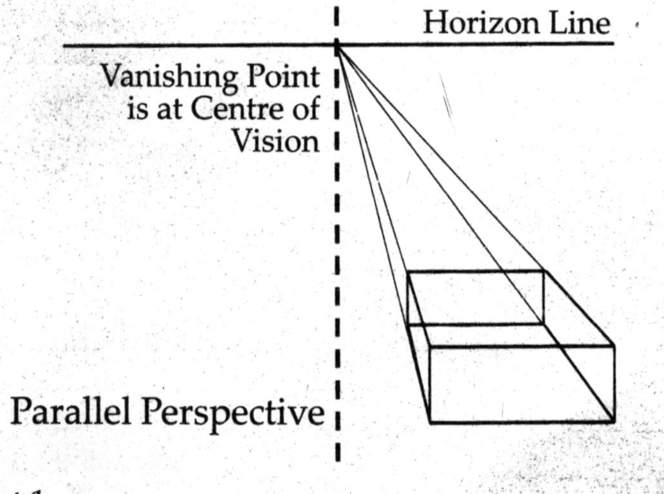

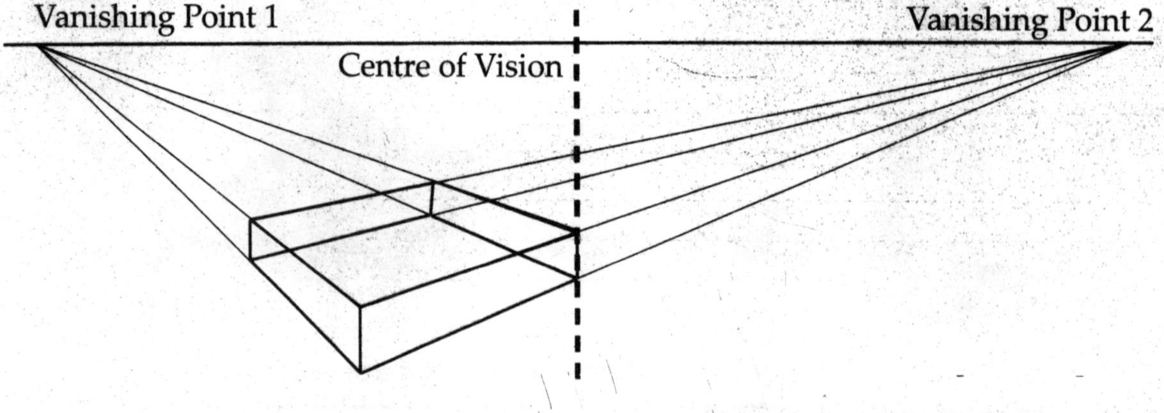

STEP-BY-STEP DRAWING

Based on the source of light, character study would require an understanding of rendering light, middle-light & dark tones to achieve a 3-dimensional effect. The drawings below amplify this. Manmade & Natural objects are fascinating due to their individual character (shape of object and features, texture of surface, colour of fruit). These features can be illustrated through shading techniques. We can trace printed pictures from magazines for practice.

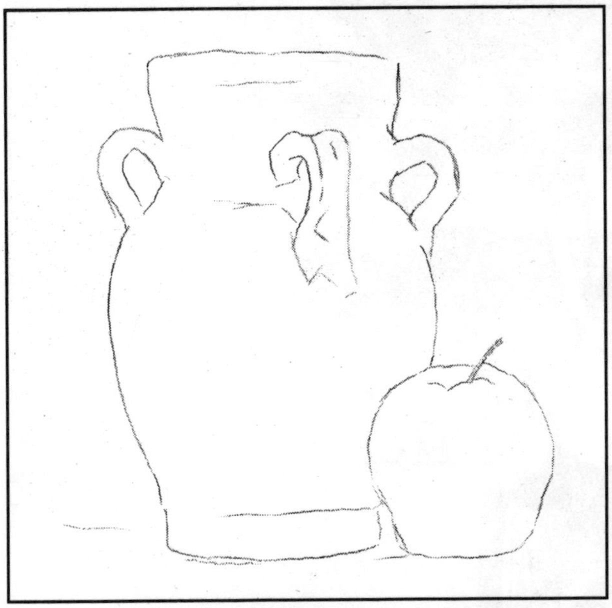

Draw a neat clean outline contour drawing.

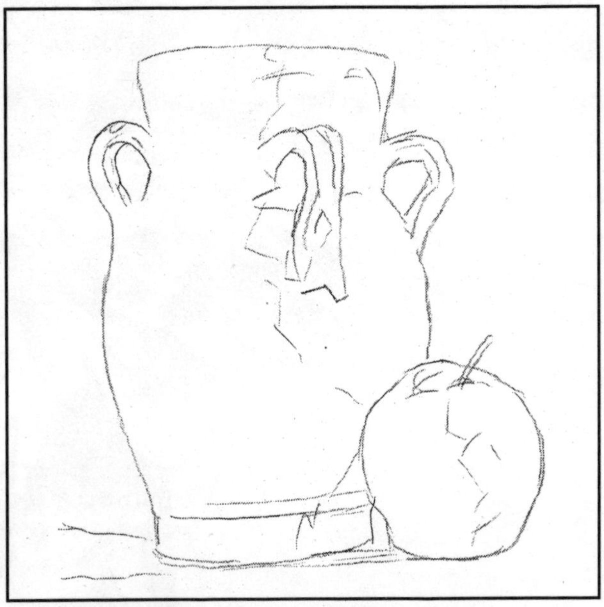

Add lines to emphasize and define details to suggest volume.

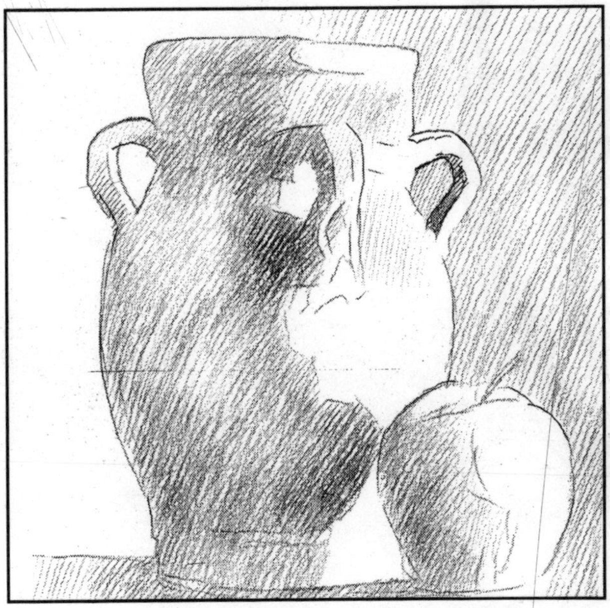

Add the tonal value to define dimensions using cross hatching.

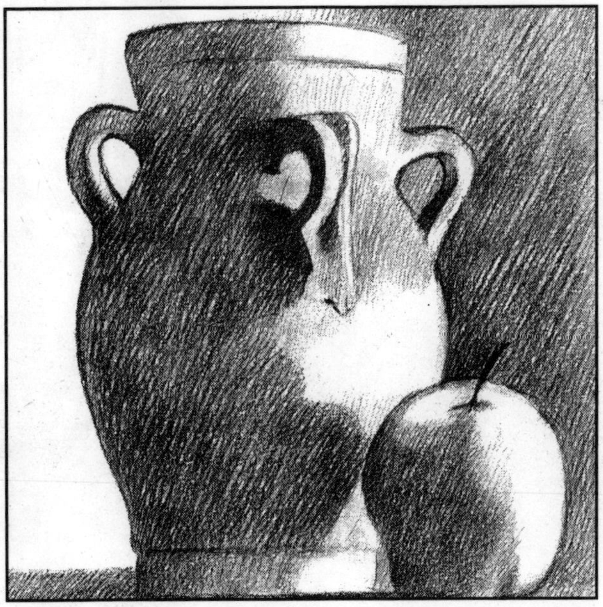

Deepen tonal value in certain areas to bring about depth and create highlights.

To convey the complexities of form, glass and petal texture, and material, vary pressure and use hatching in different directions.

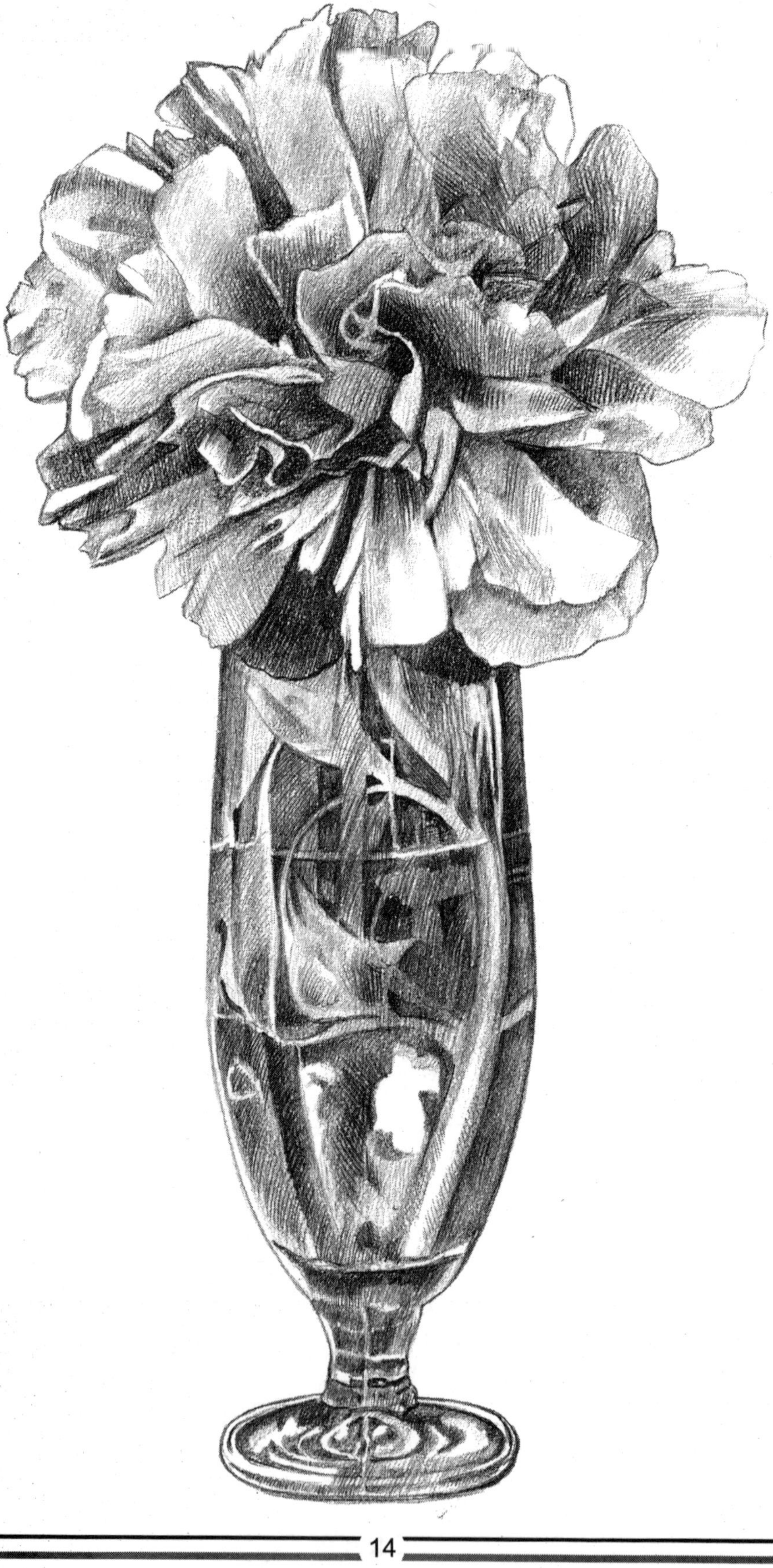

Use long strokes to express the form of the vase and flower.

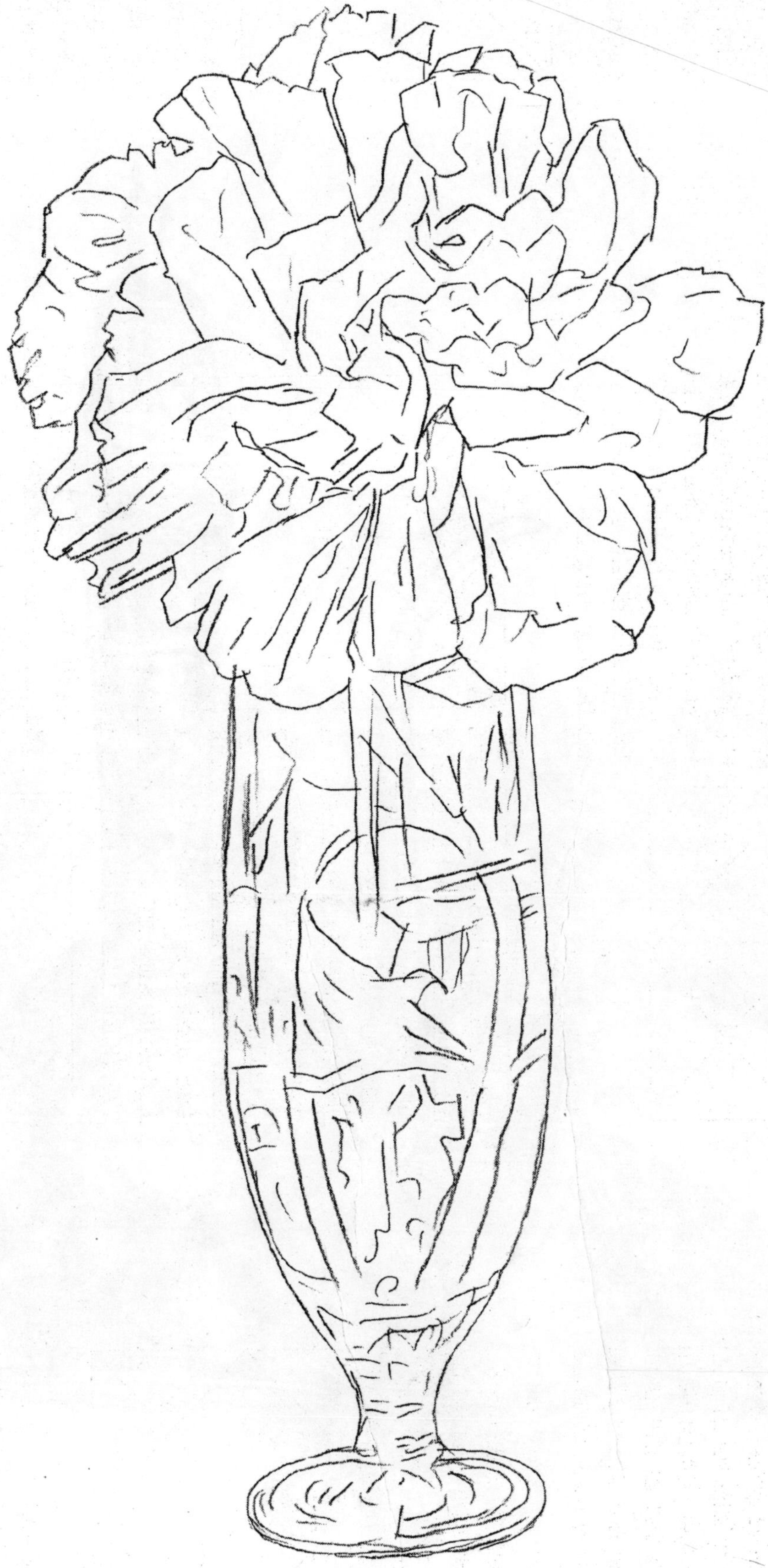

Observe the deep tones that bring out the metallic character of the jar.
The shapes of highlights are also important.

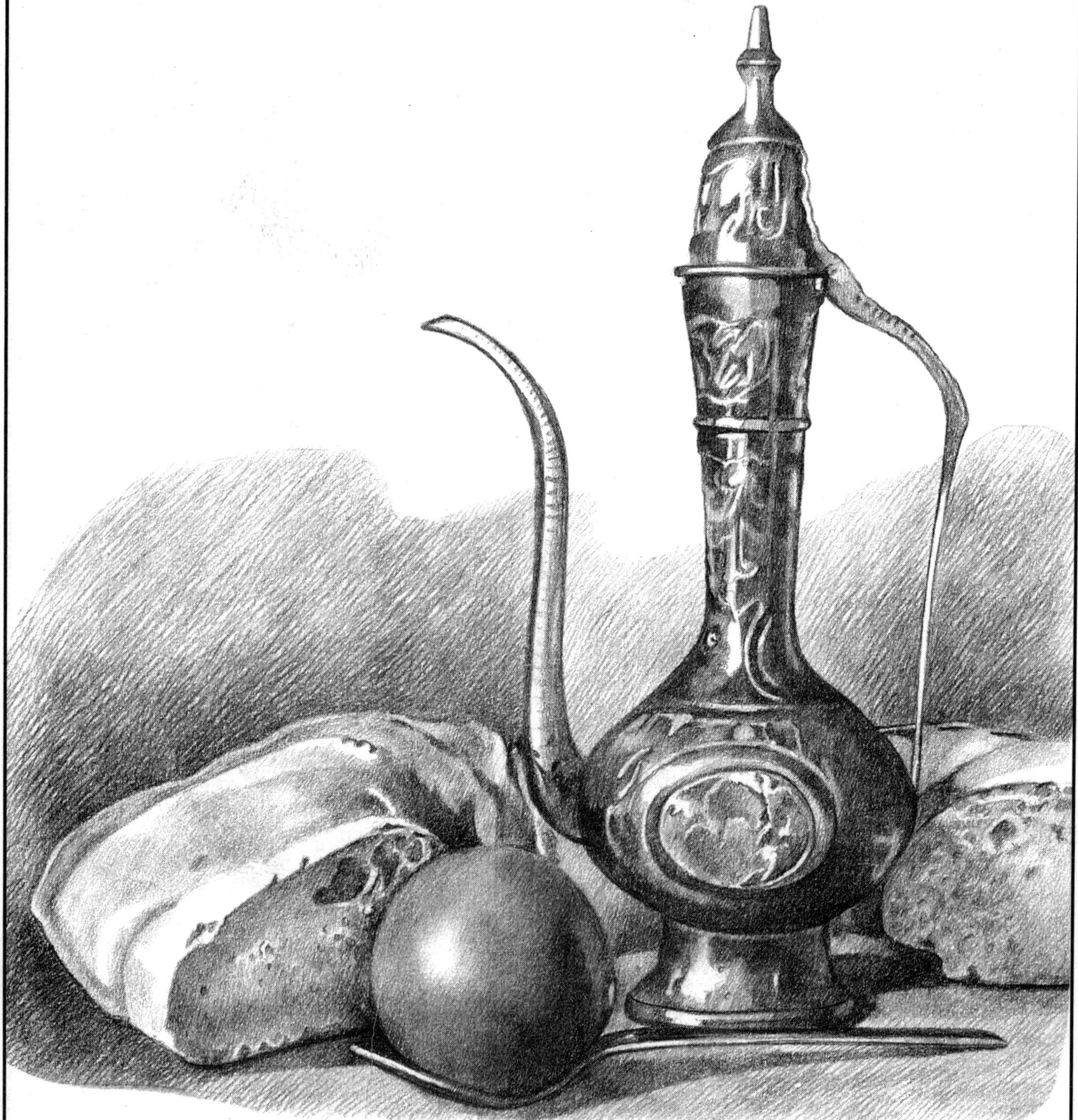

Draw the lines for highlights and the relief work on the metal jar carefully.

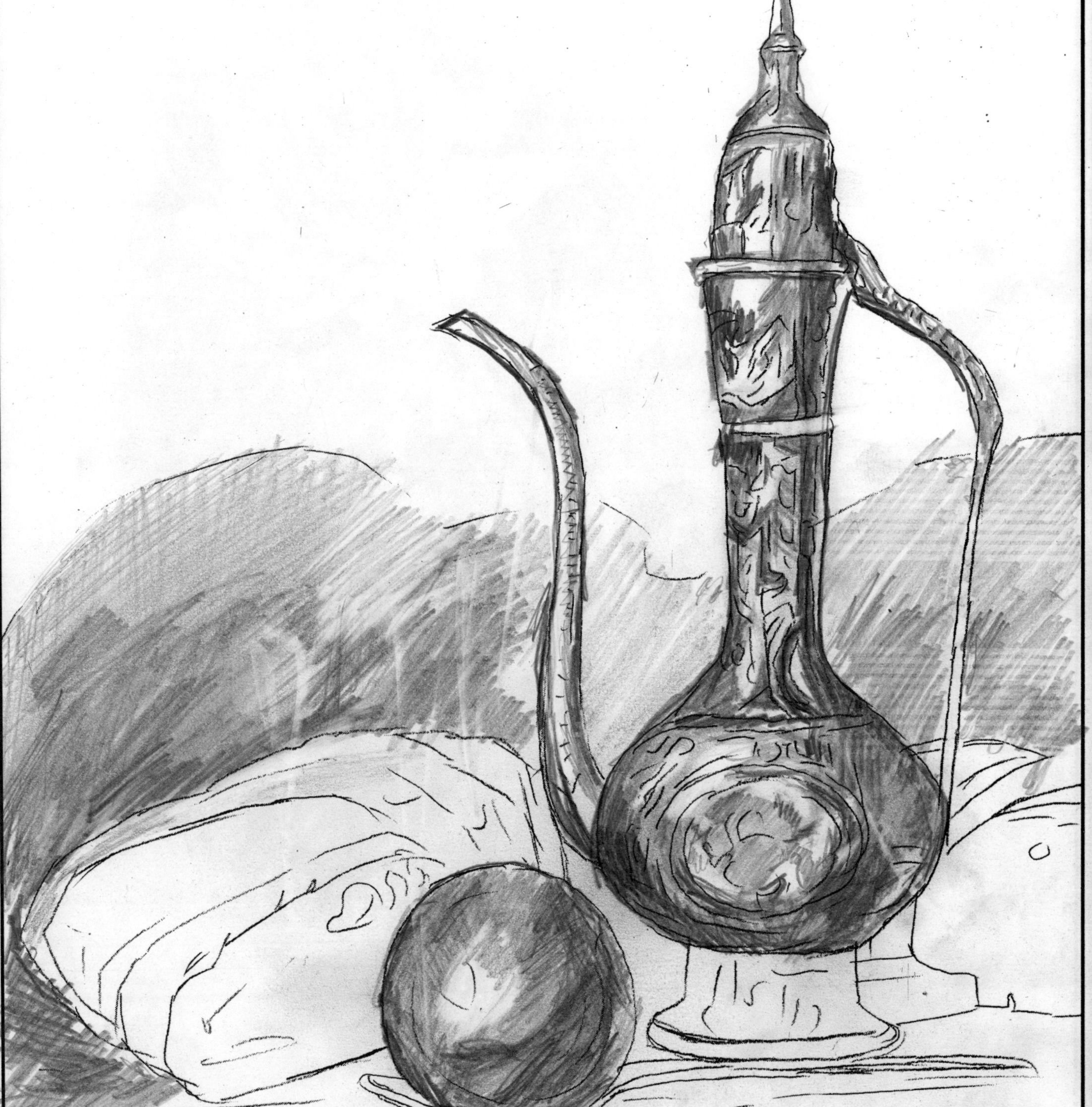

Observe the difference in the texture of the petals and the leaves. Hatch in different directions as per the shape of the object.

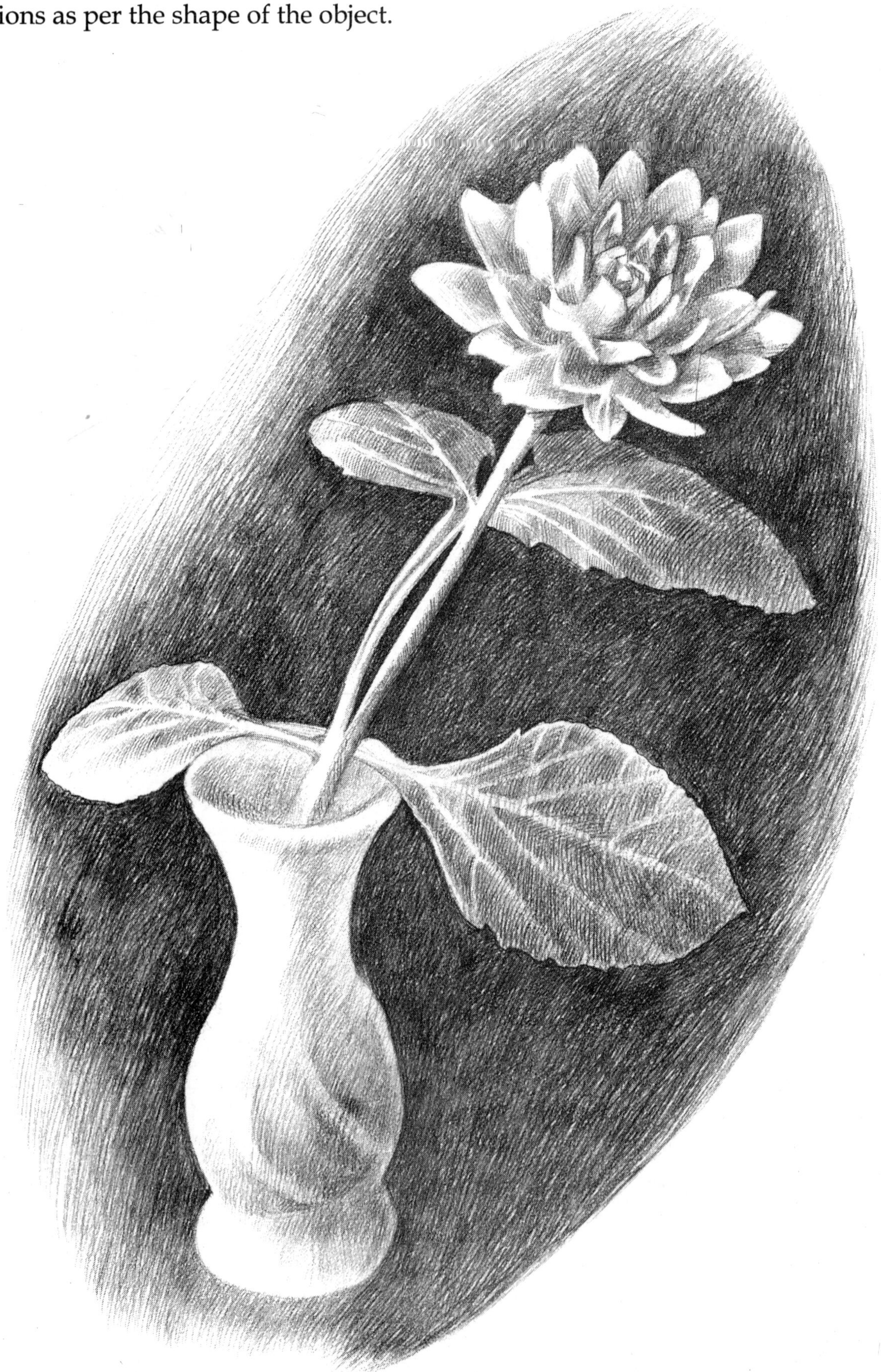

Observe the detailed lines of the flower so that you can bring out the form while shading.

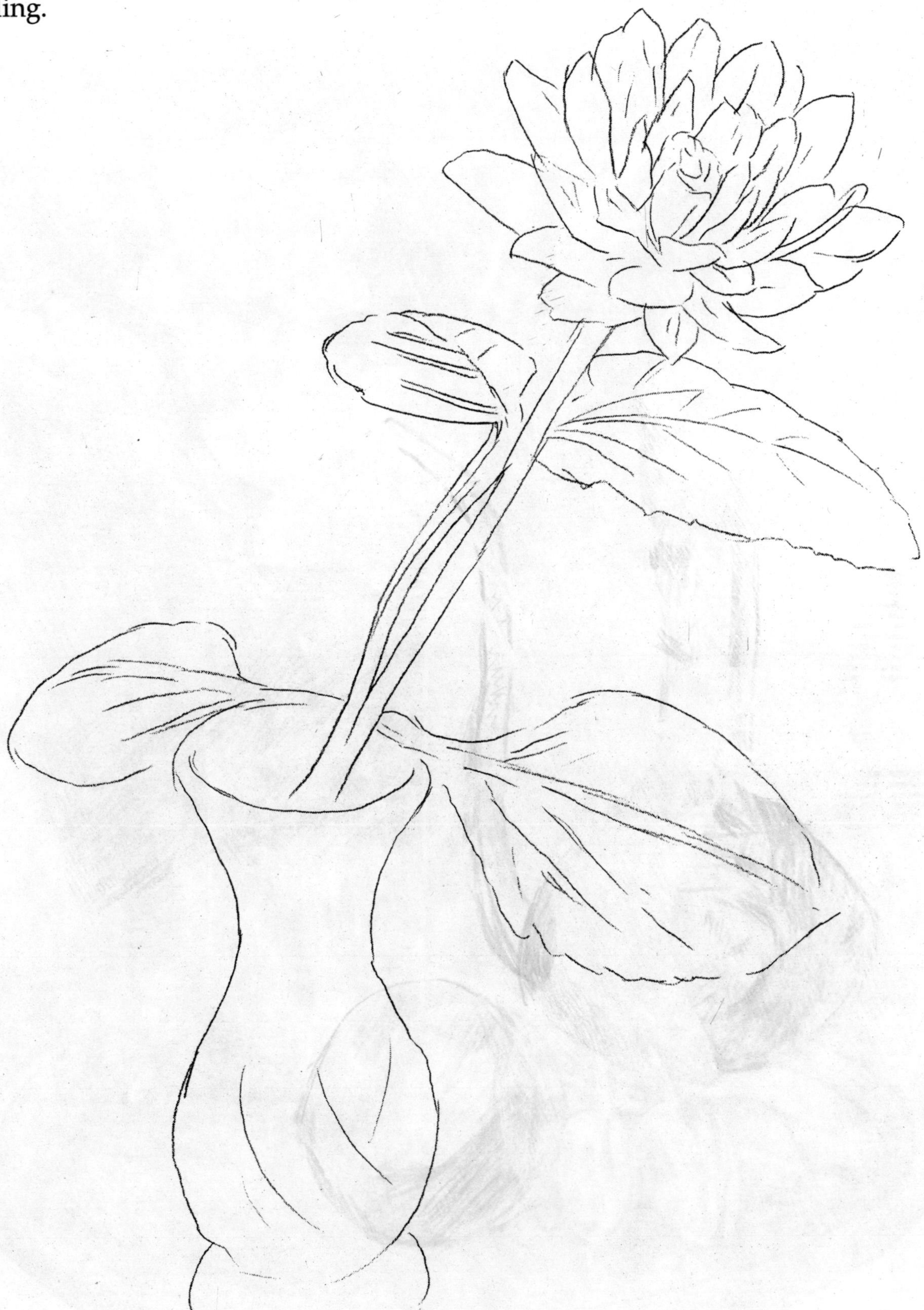

The dark shading of the background gives depth to this still life.

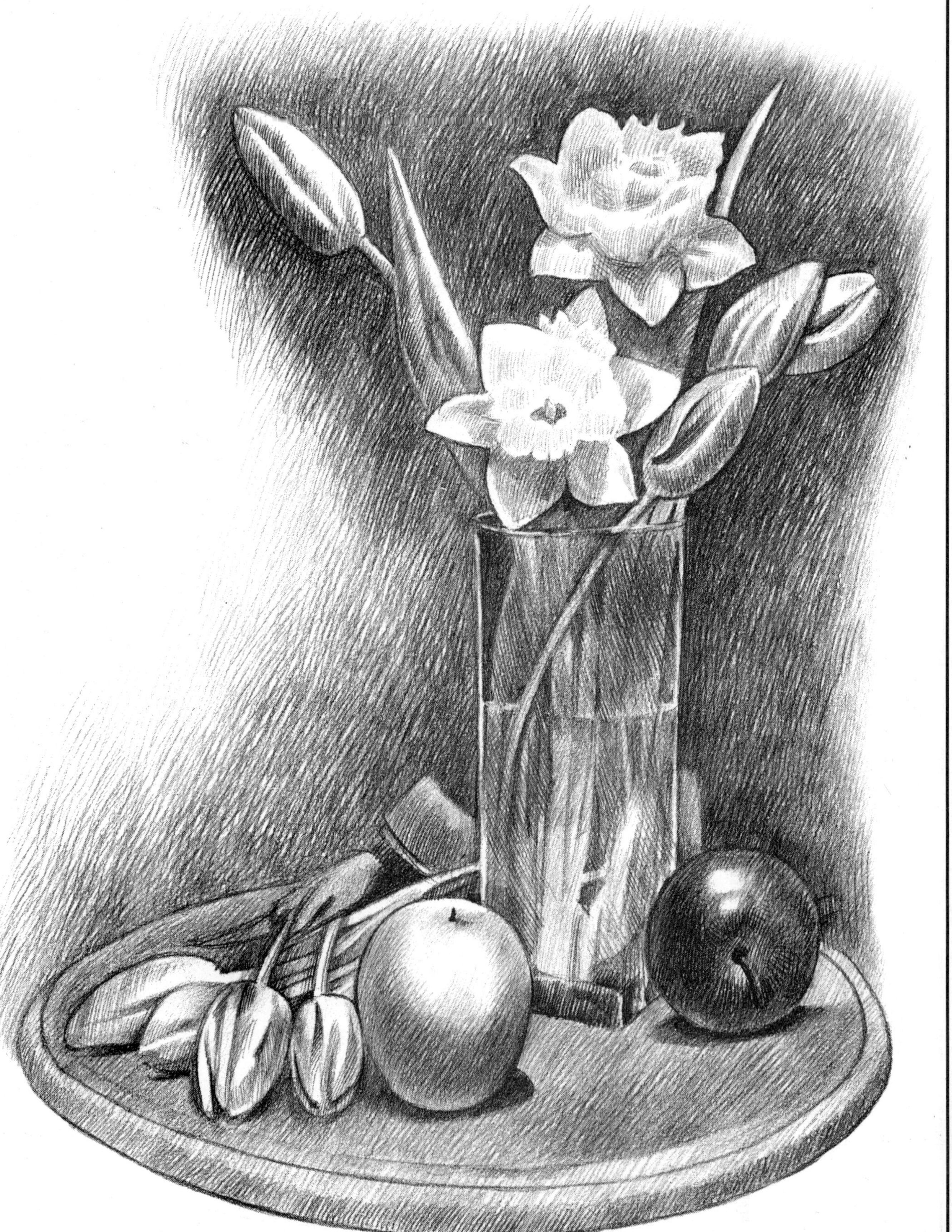

Observe the composition and placement of objects that make this arrangement interesting.

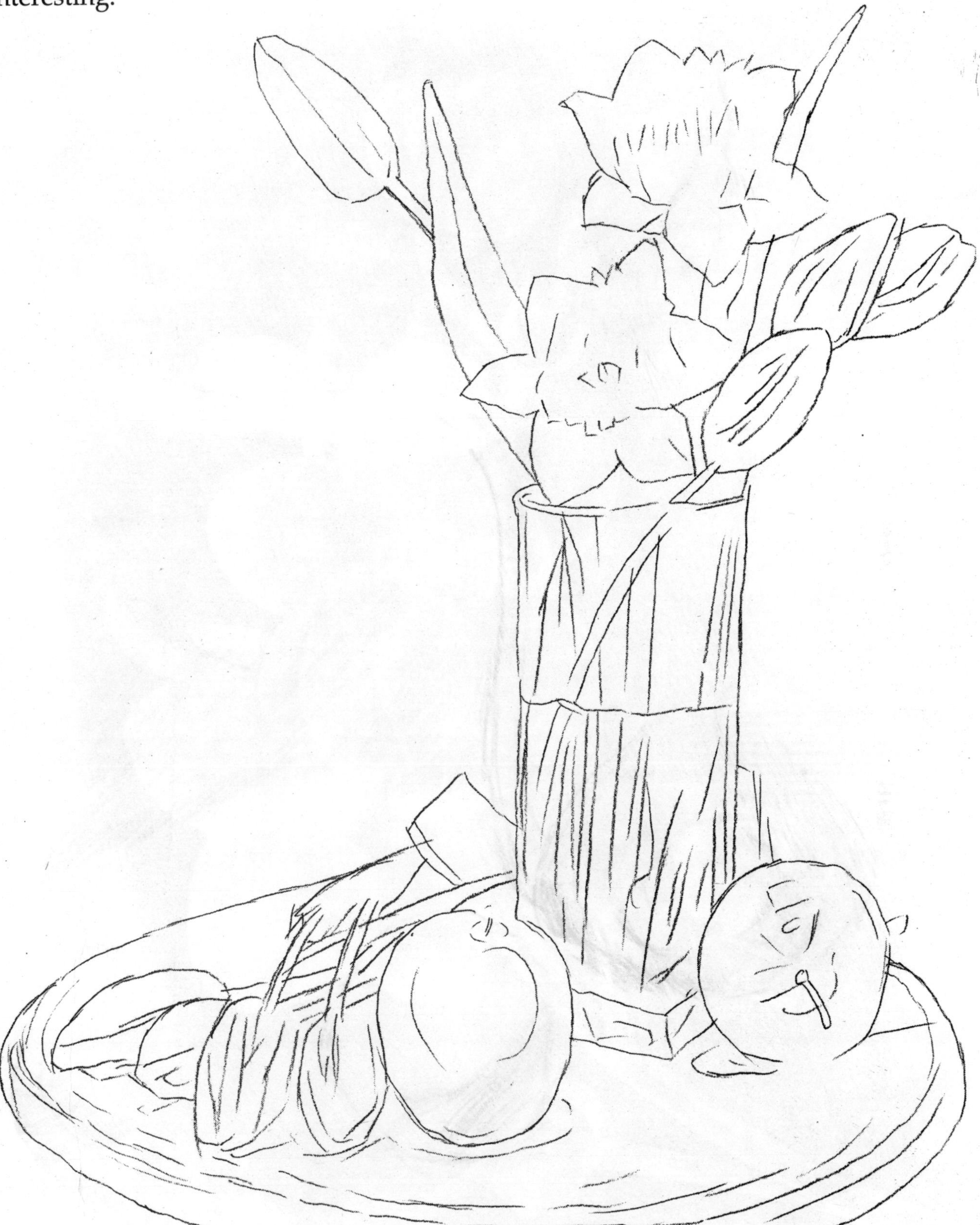

Observe the highlights and the middle tonal shade that gives the blossom its form.

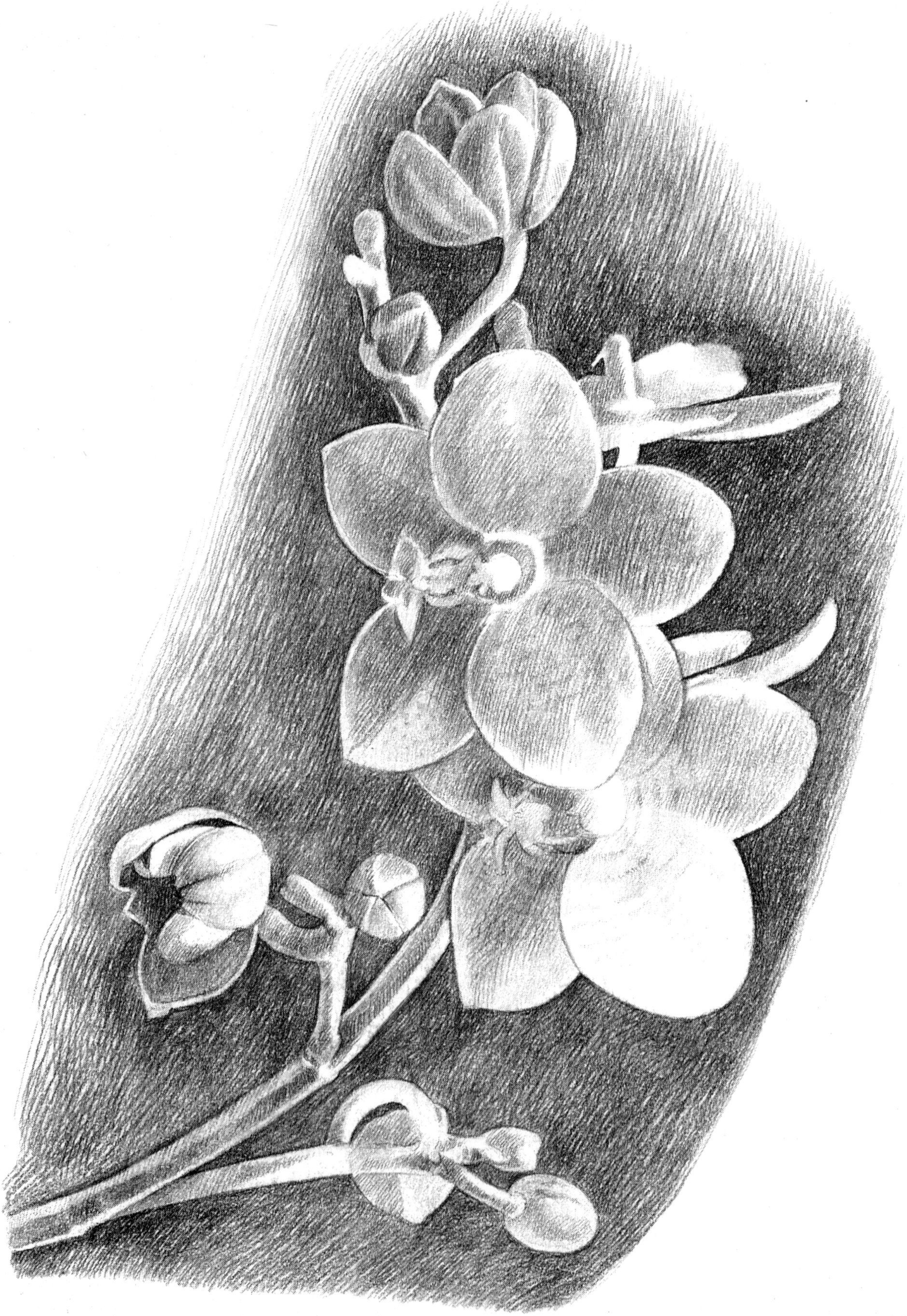

The details of the drawing of all the shades and highlights are to be marked carefully to make shading easy.

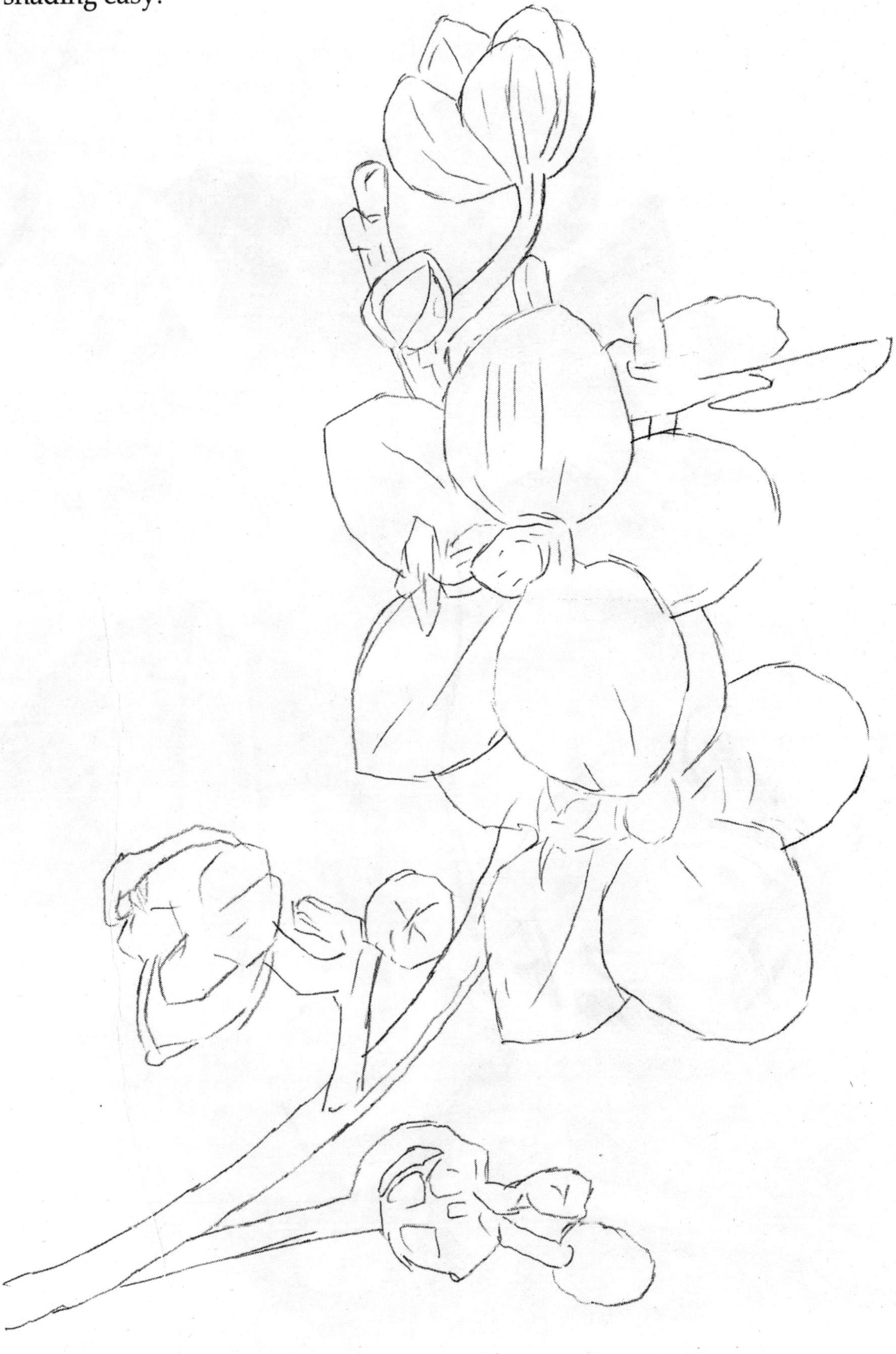

To get tonal values of this white colour tea set first apply even strokes with hatching style, then smudge with paper stump, then render dark areas with cross hatching.

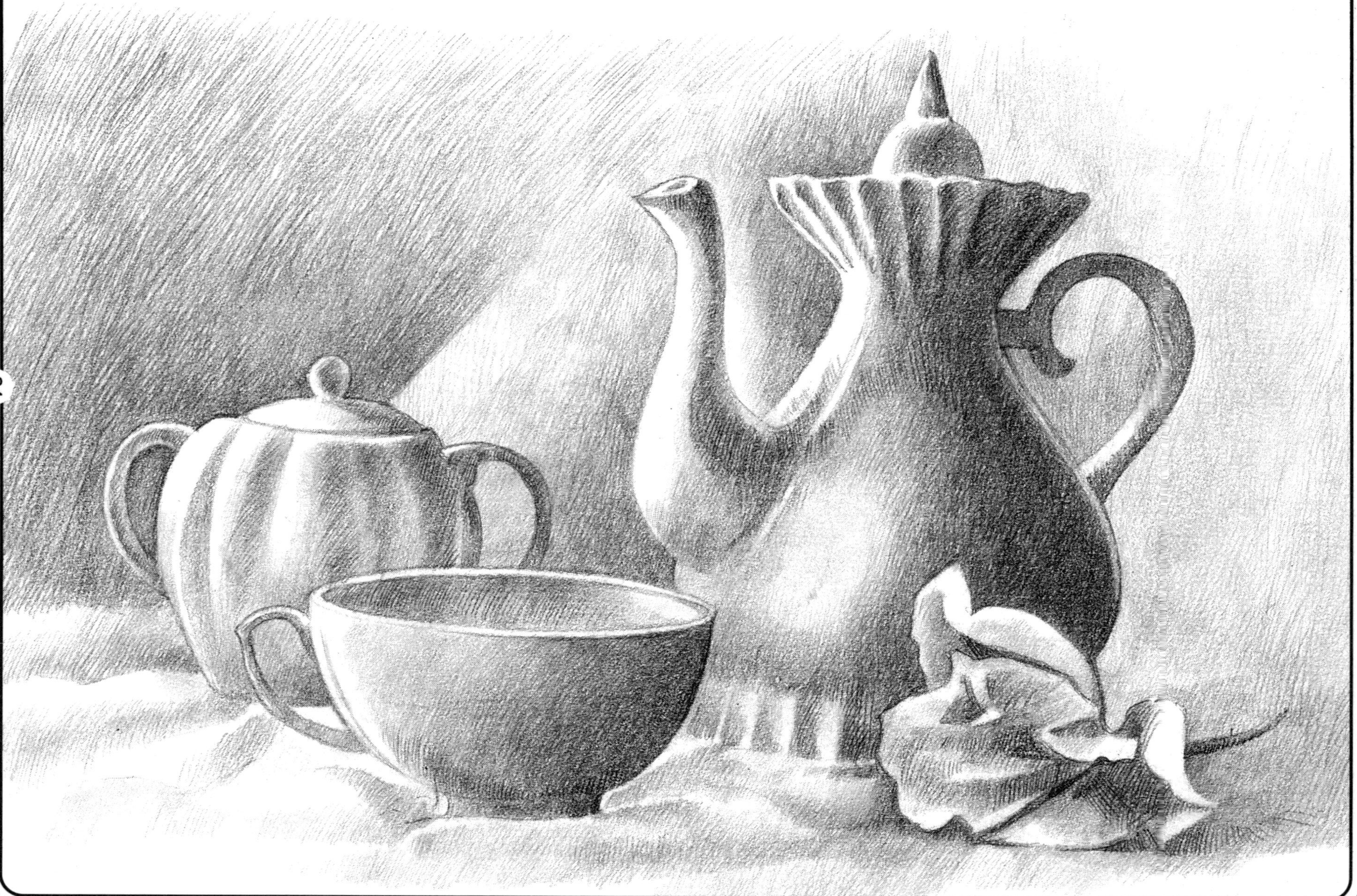

Draw a neat clean contour drawing observing the perspectives of the cup and the kettle.

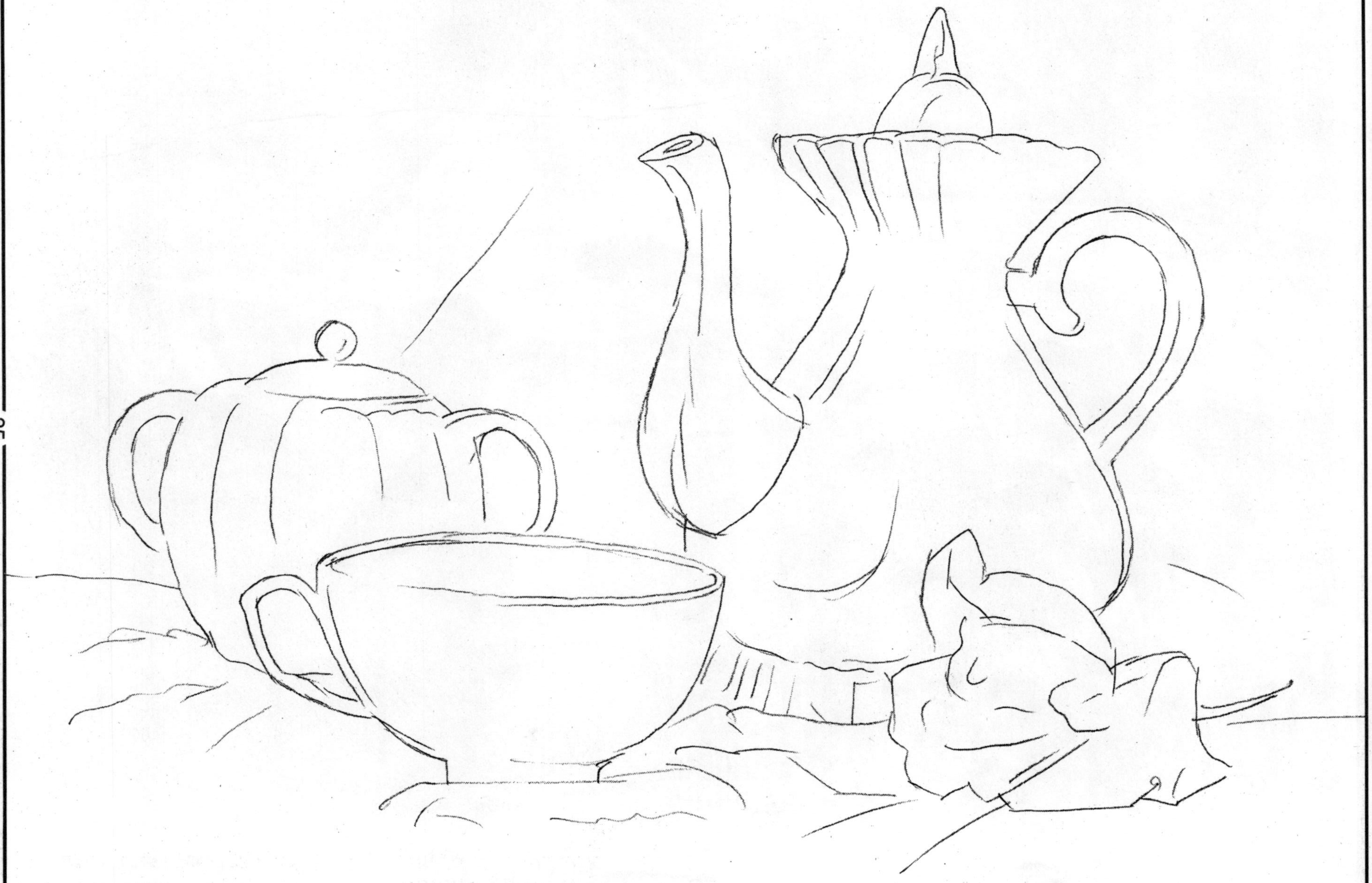

Tonal values are added to define the folds of the cloth using cross hatching in the directions of the folds.

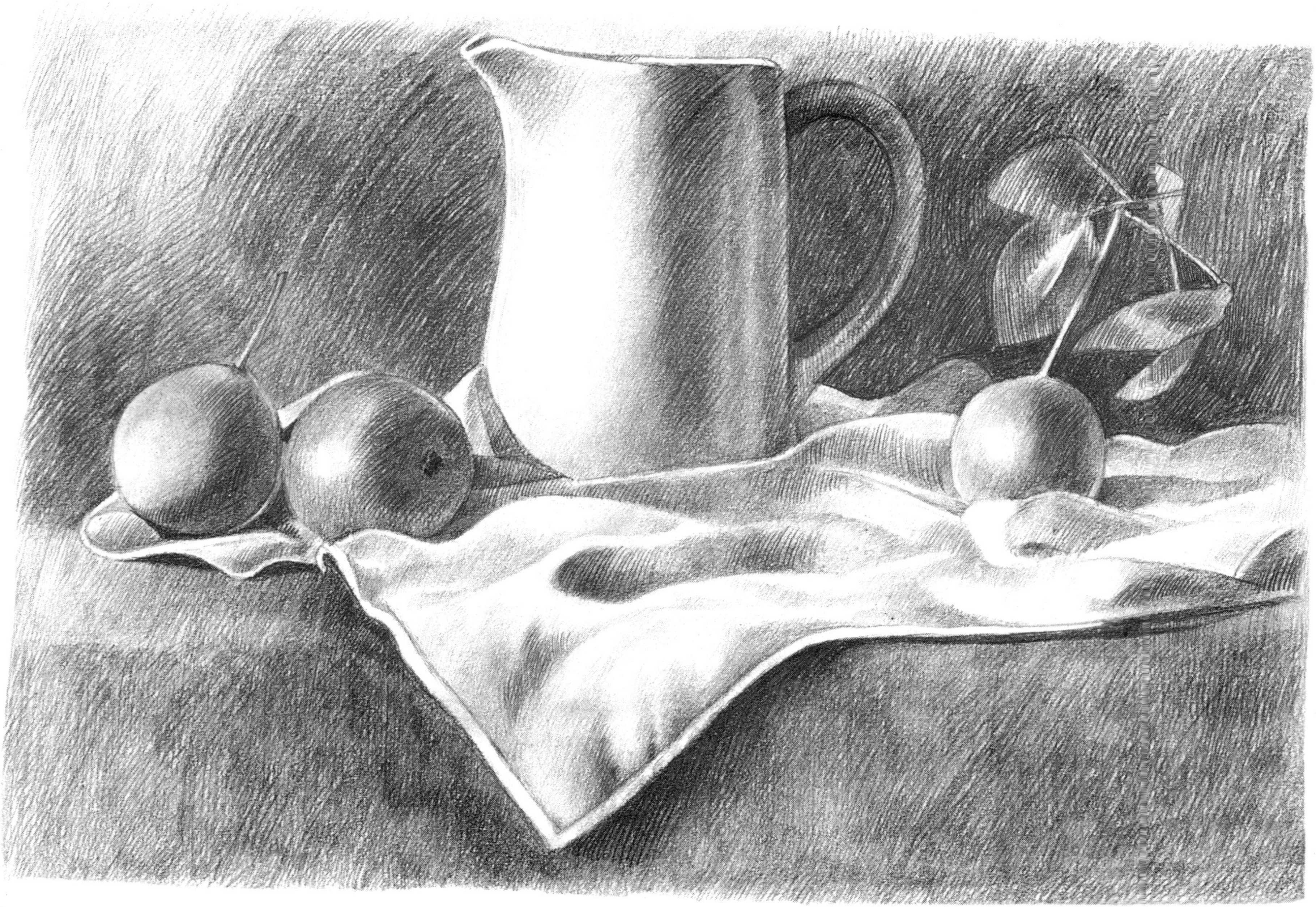

Draw the details of the folds and the fruits with care.

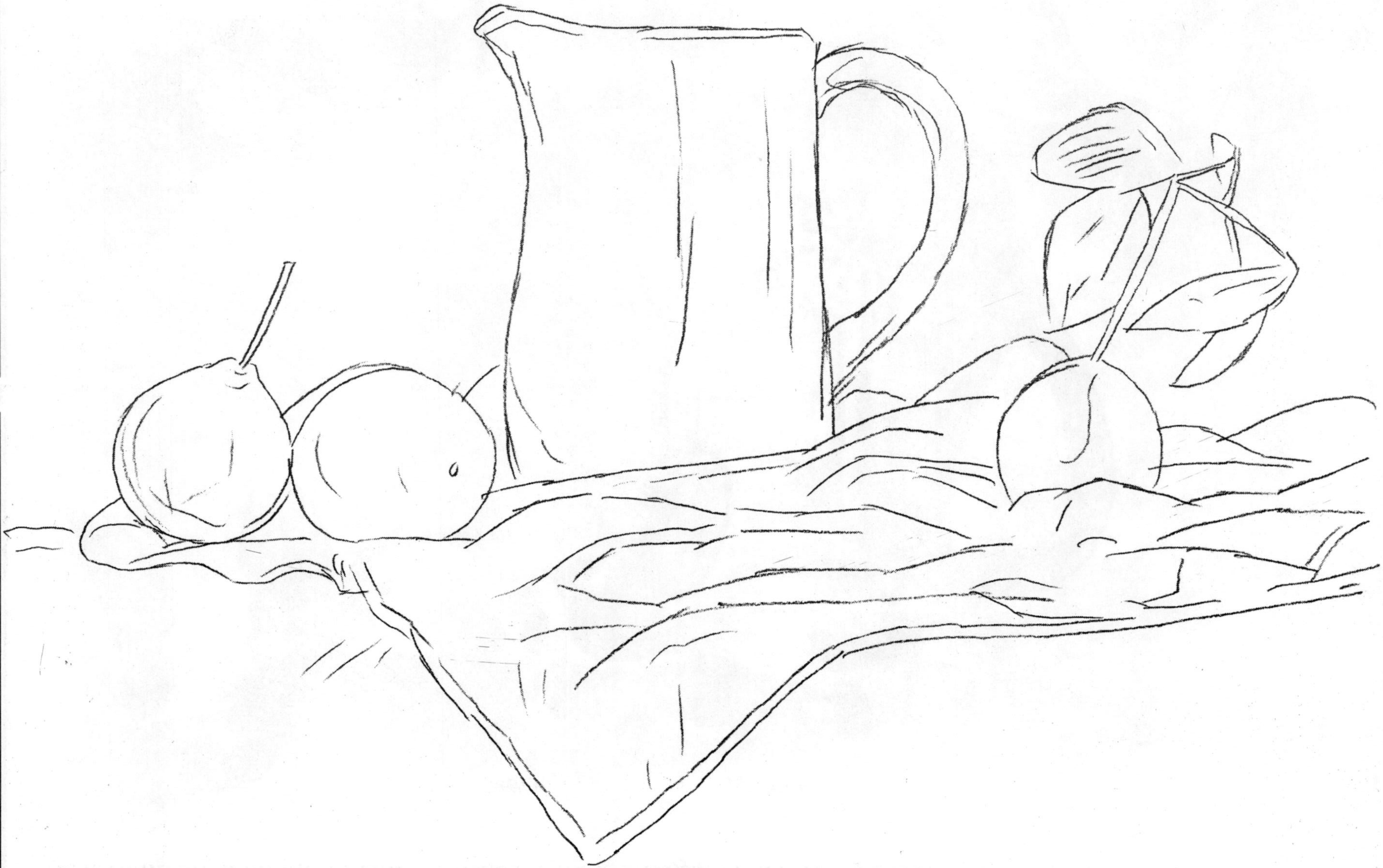

Observe the light on the jar and the fruits, there is a bright light from one direction.

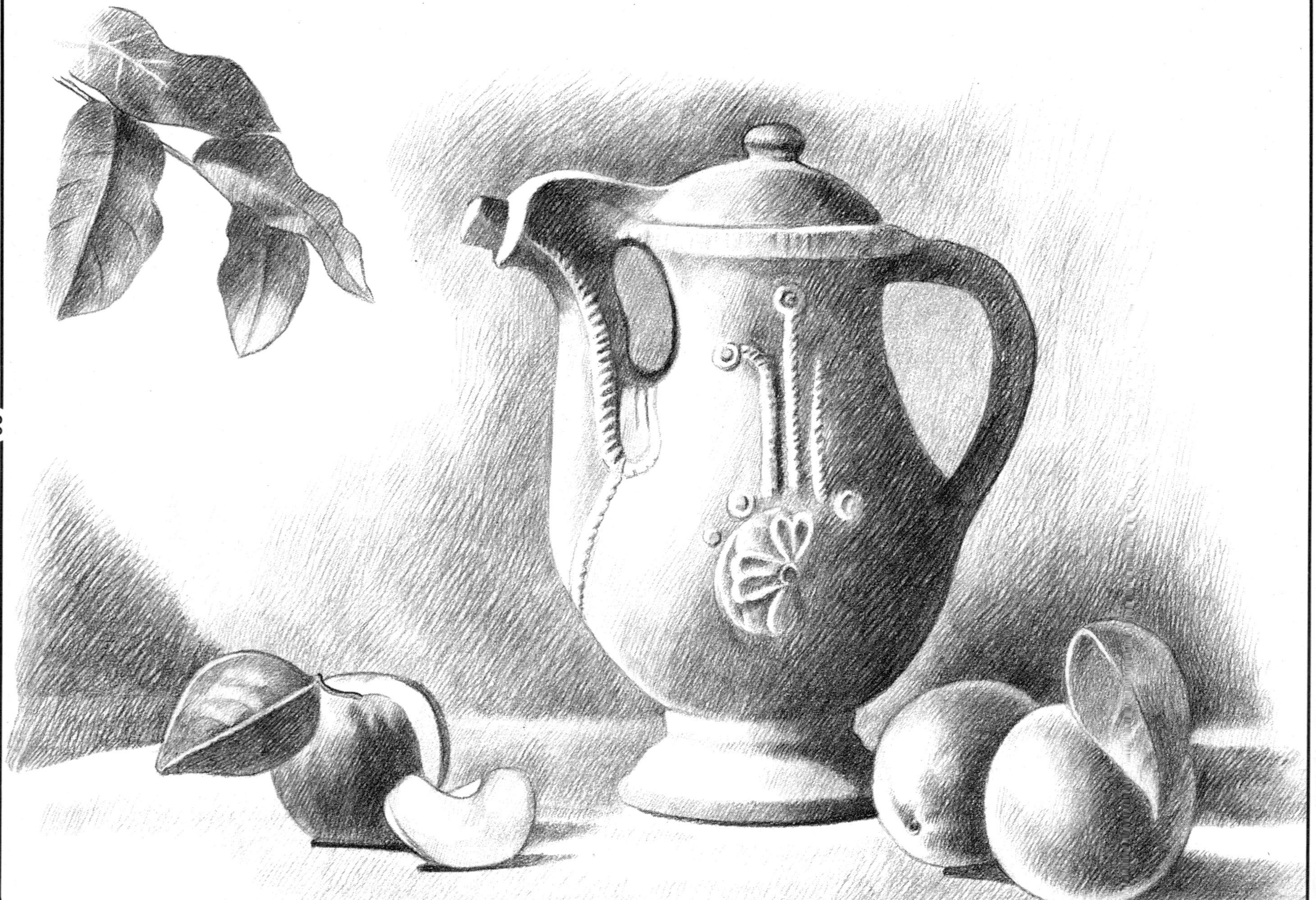

Carefully draw the relief work on the jar.

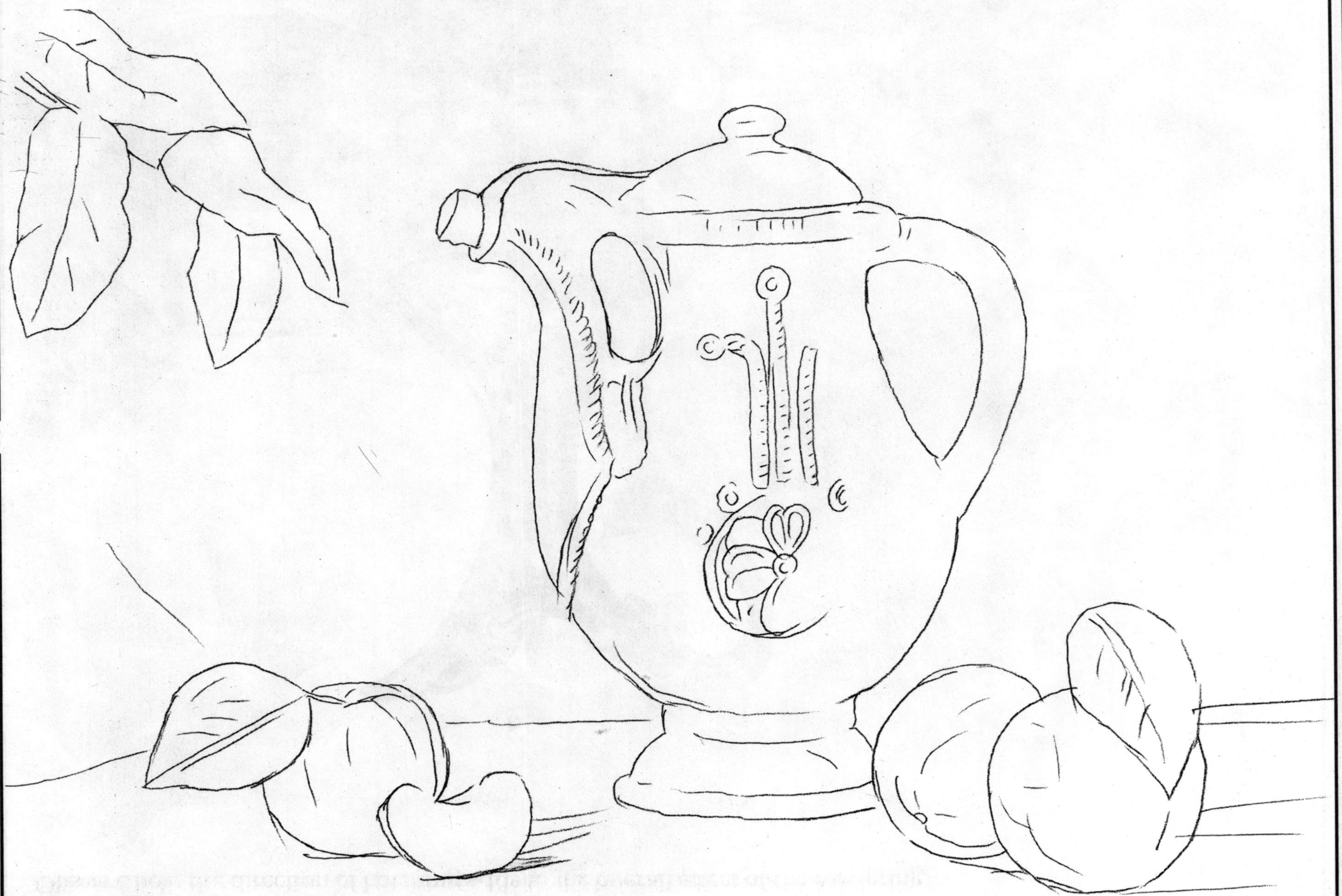

Observe how the direction of hatching adds to the overall effect of the rendering.

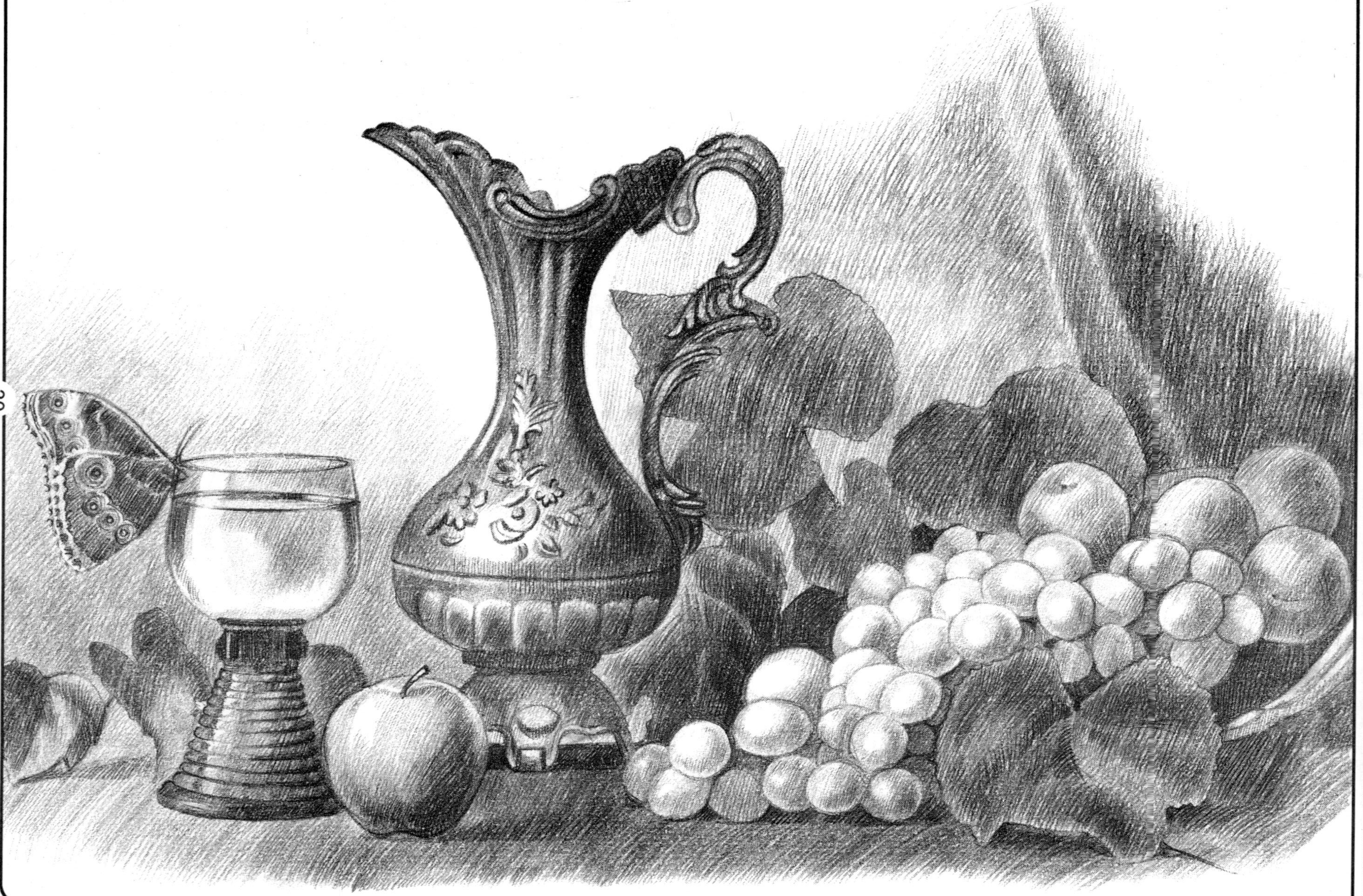

Draw the details on the jar with care.

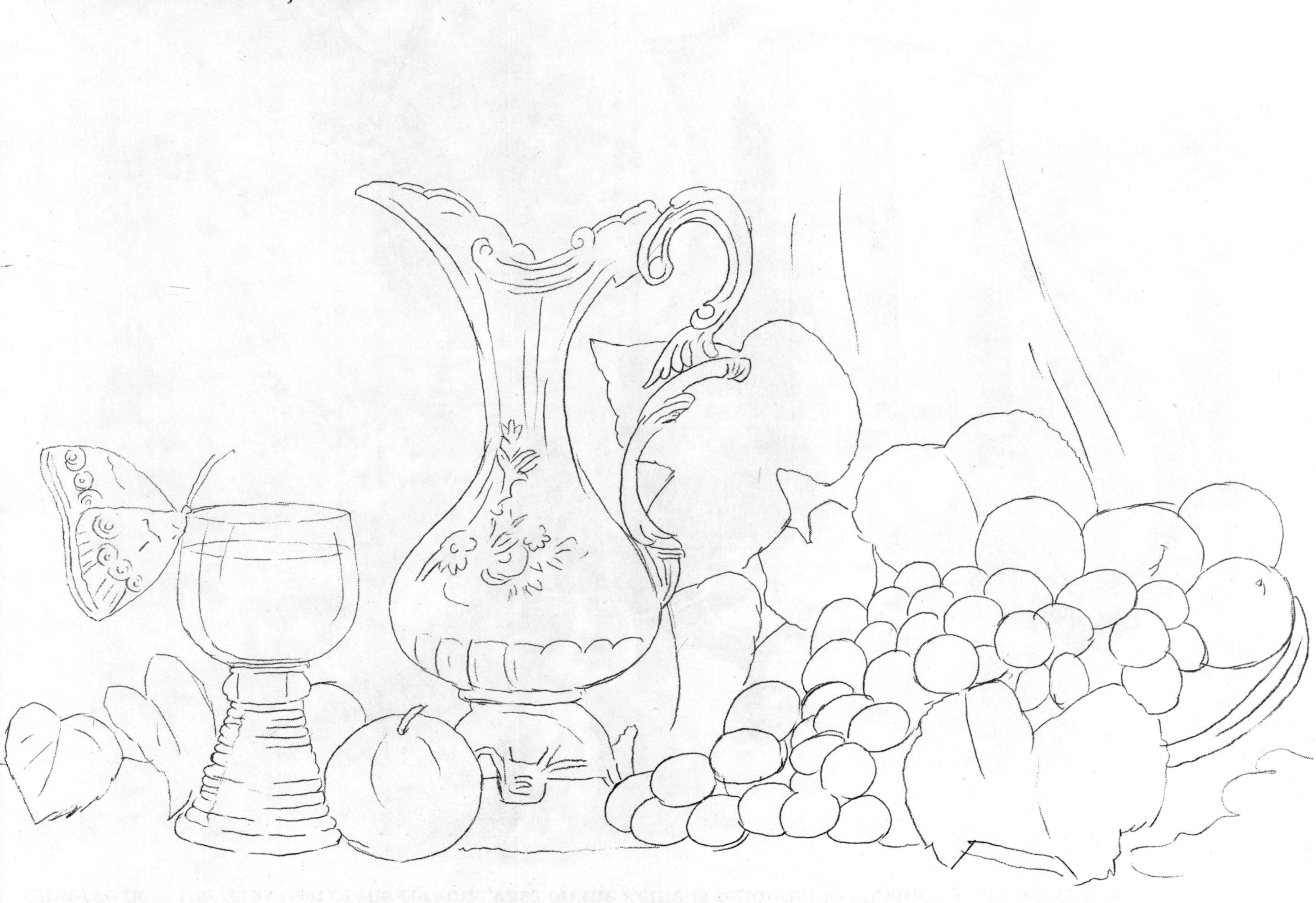

Observe how the reflection of the ceramic vase on the kettle is rendered to enhance its metallic look.

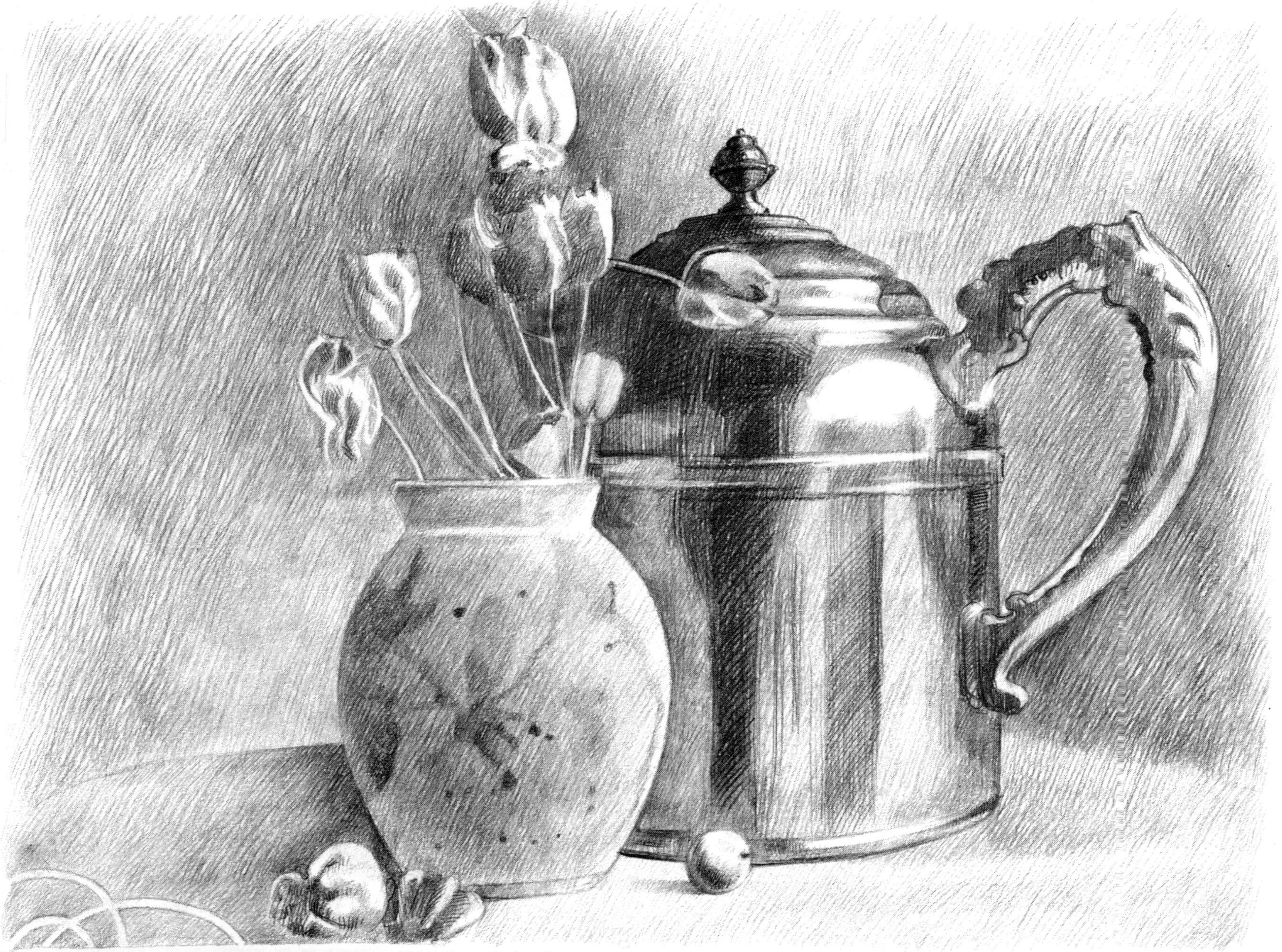

Even the most simple compositions can be very interesting due to different finishing done on the of objects.

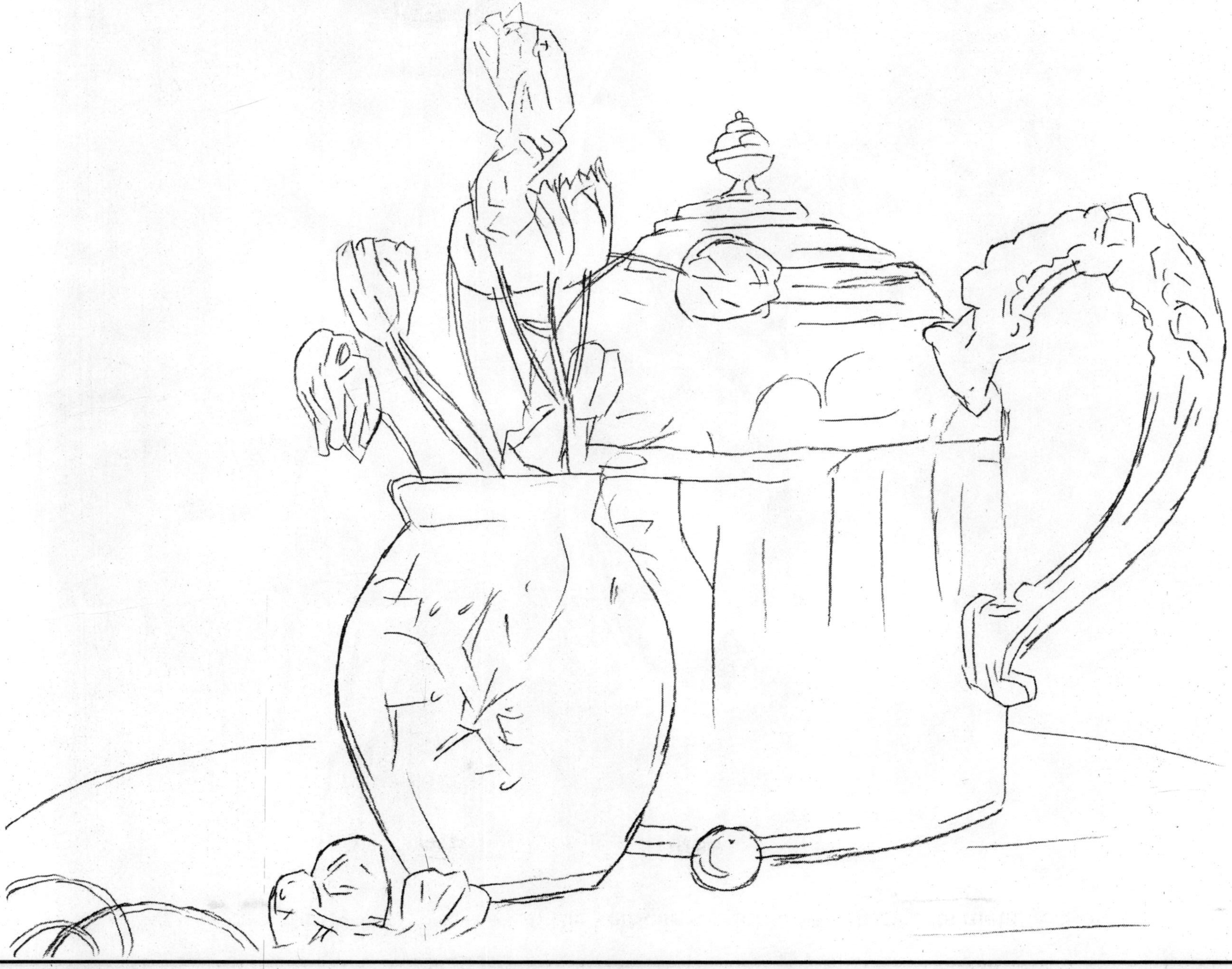

Observe the light and how it affects the form of the objects.

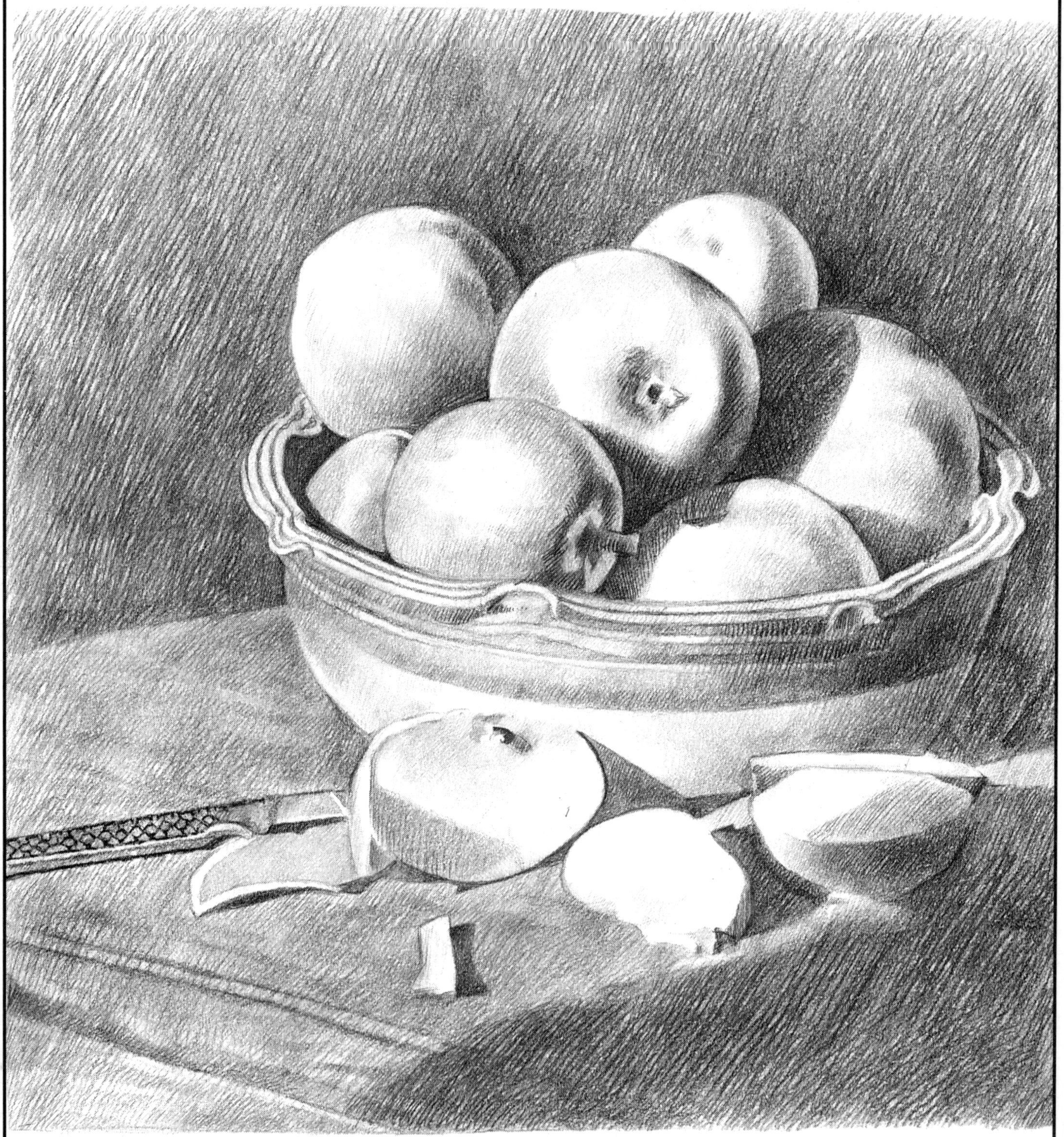

All fruits are round but still each has an individual shape, draw the contour lines to depict these differences.

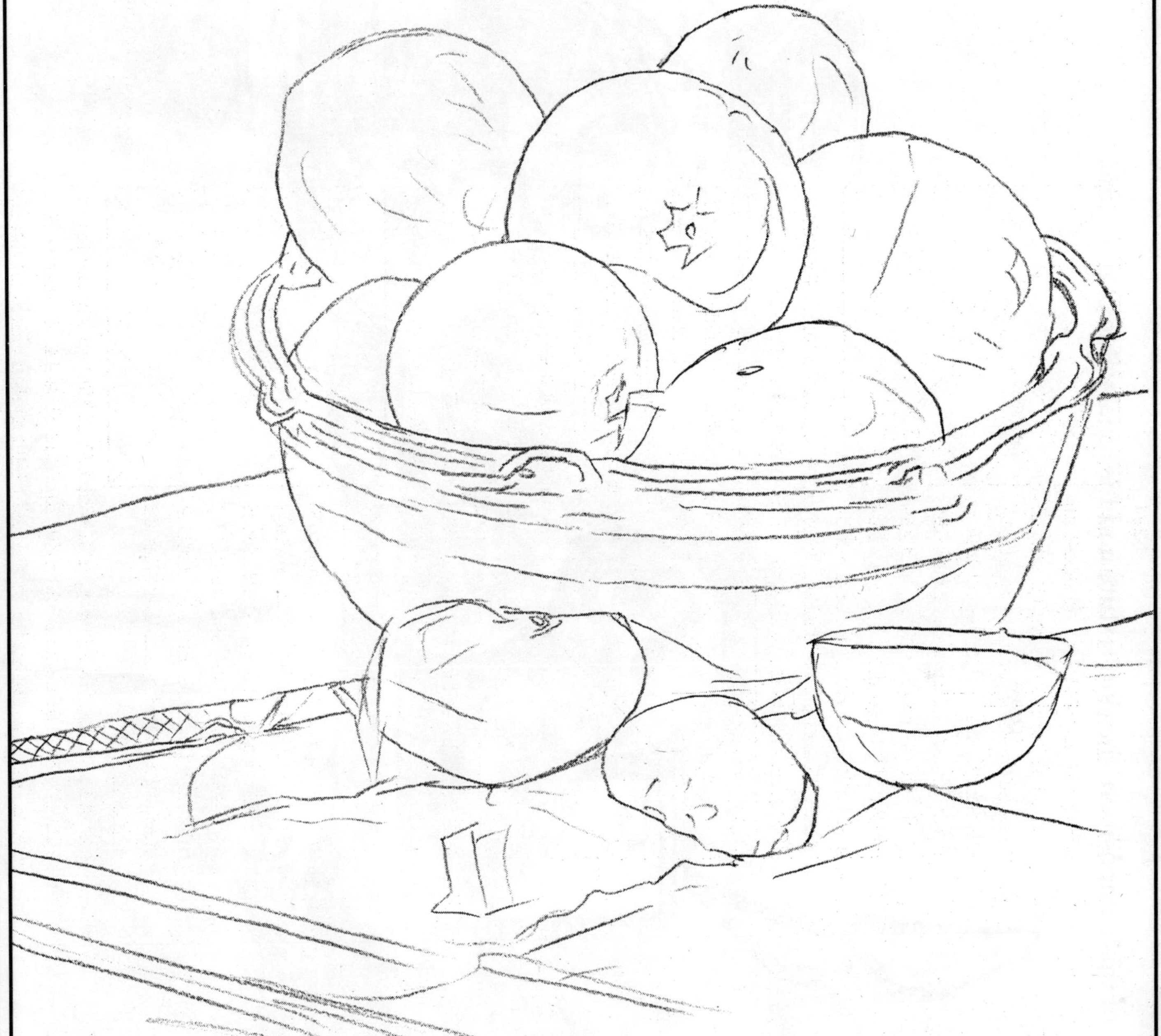

Observe the flow of this composition, the skin texture and the tonal value of the fruits.

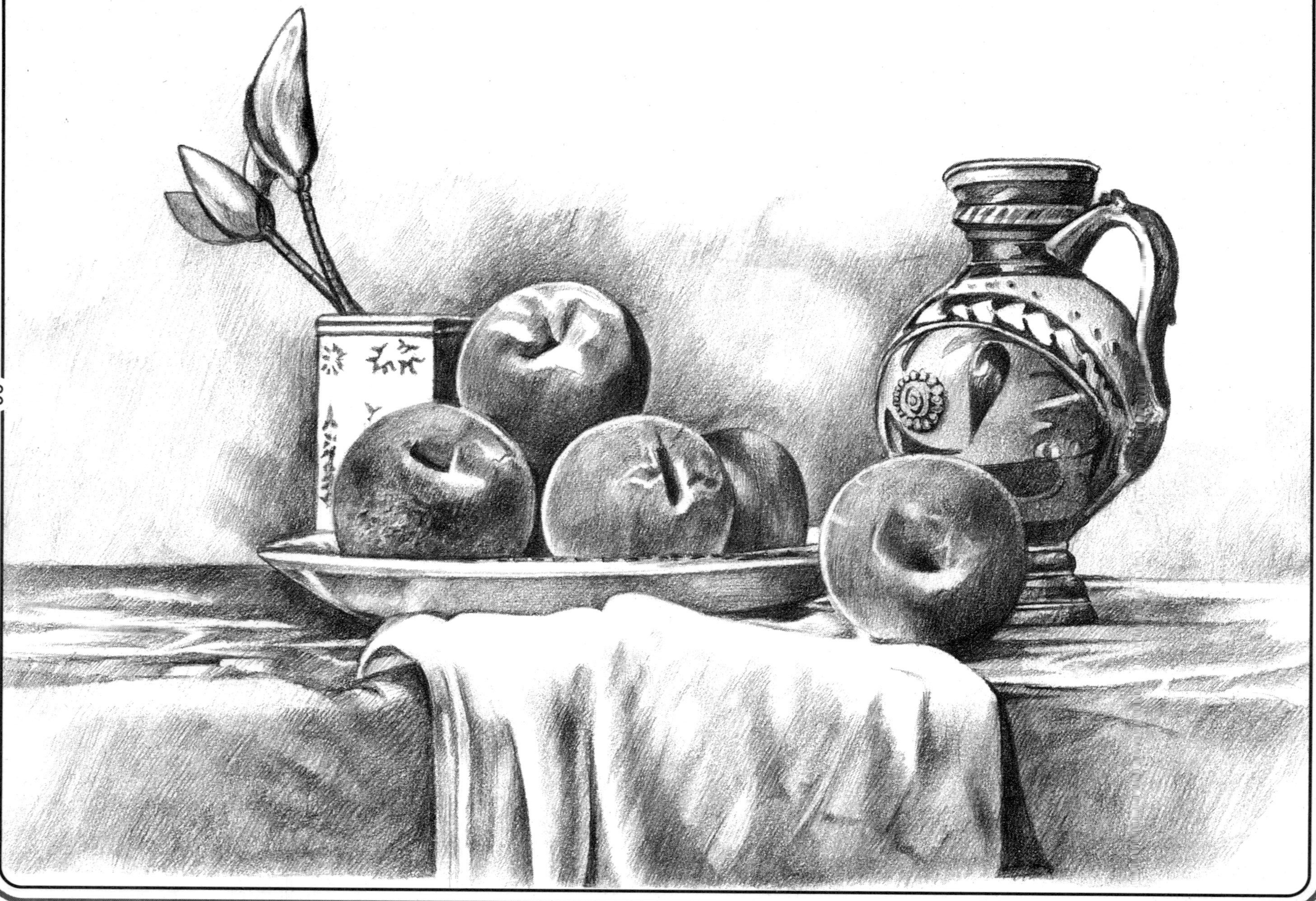

Keep in mind the flow of the cloth and the perspective while drawing.

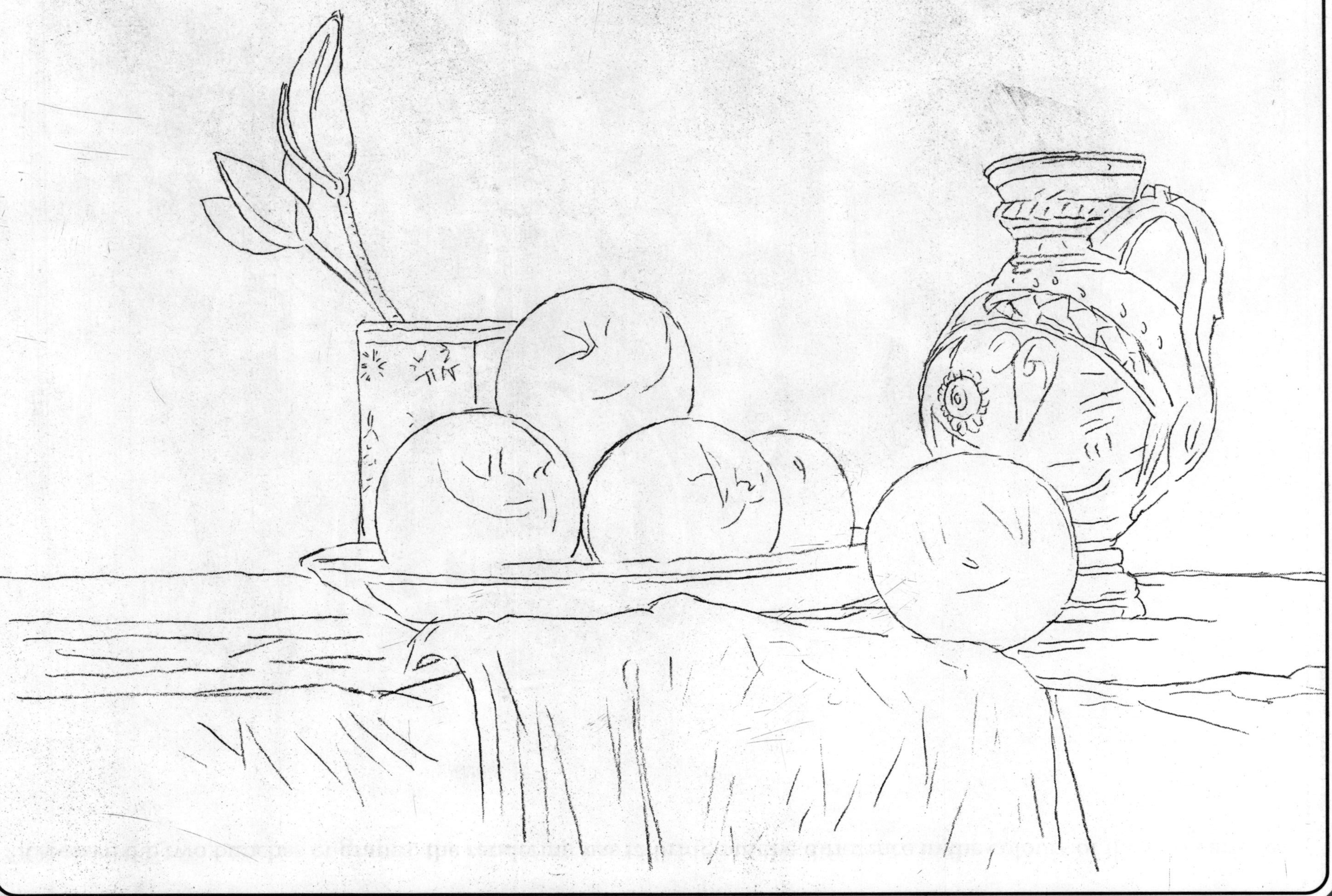

Observe the two bunches of grapes, the rendering has to bring out the difference in the colours of the two varieties.

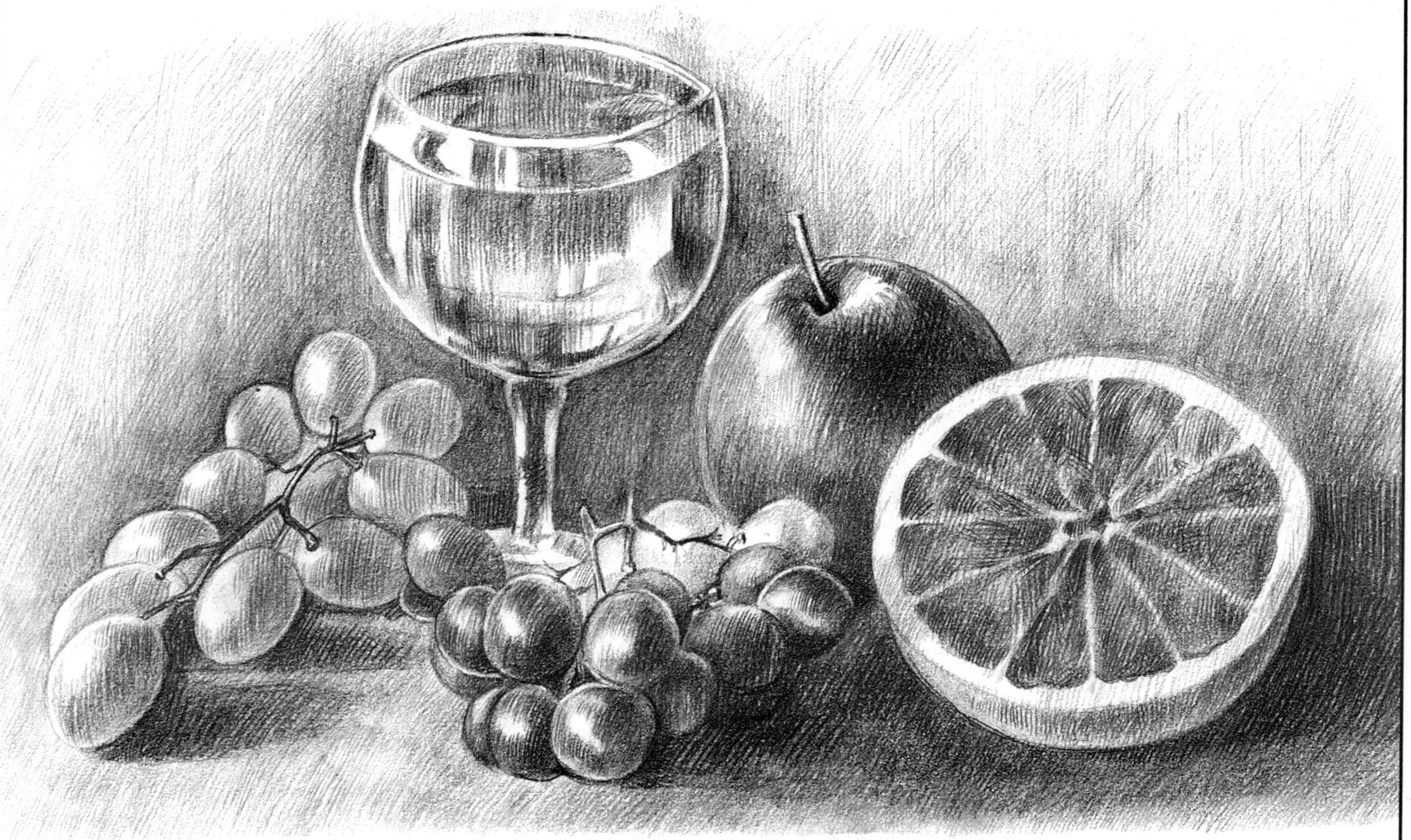

Neat clear contours will help you shade better.

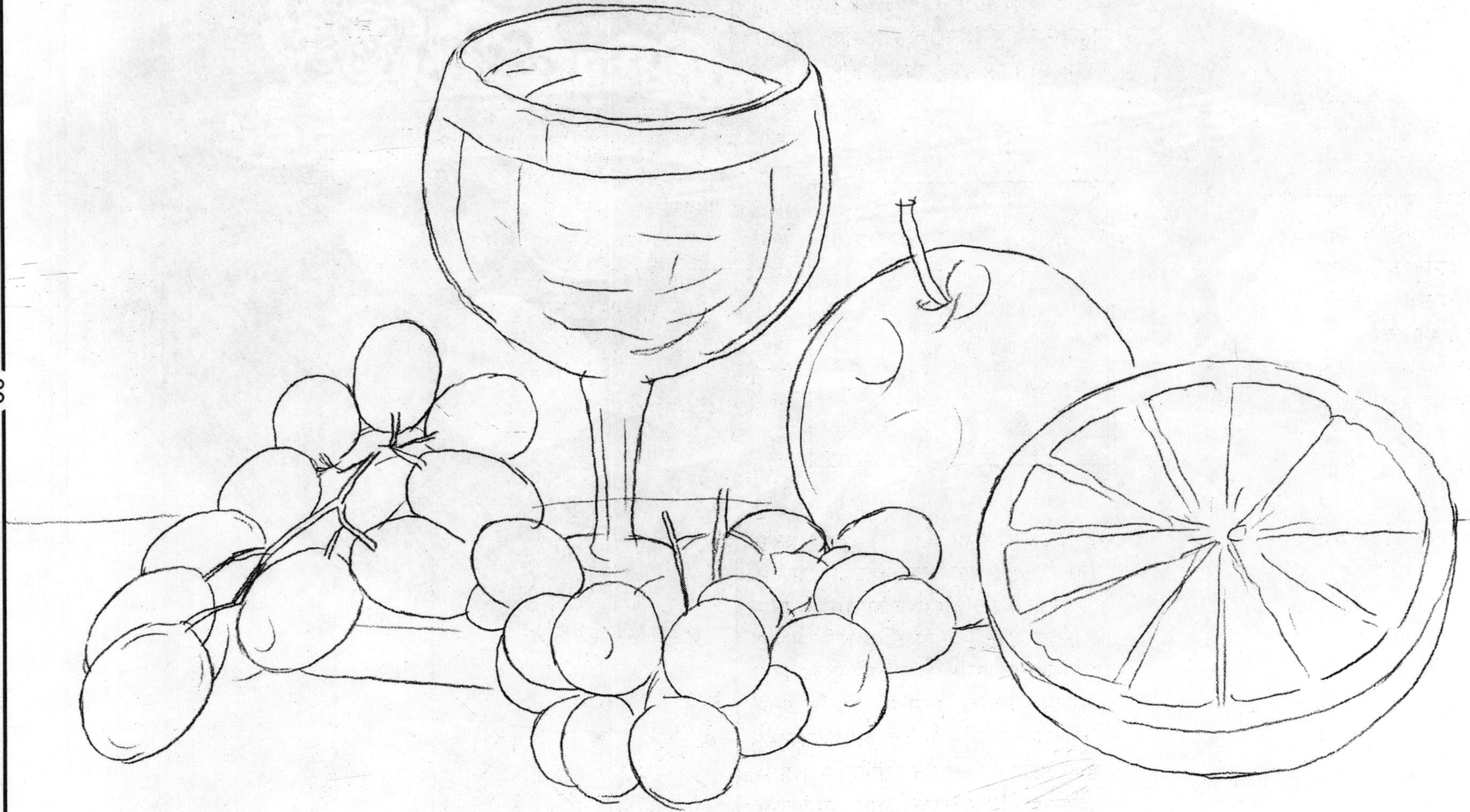

A deep background with cross hatching is used to enhance the lighter tones of the objects.

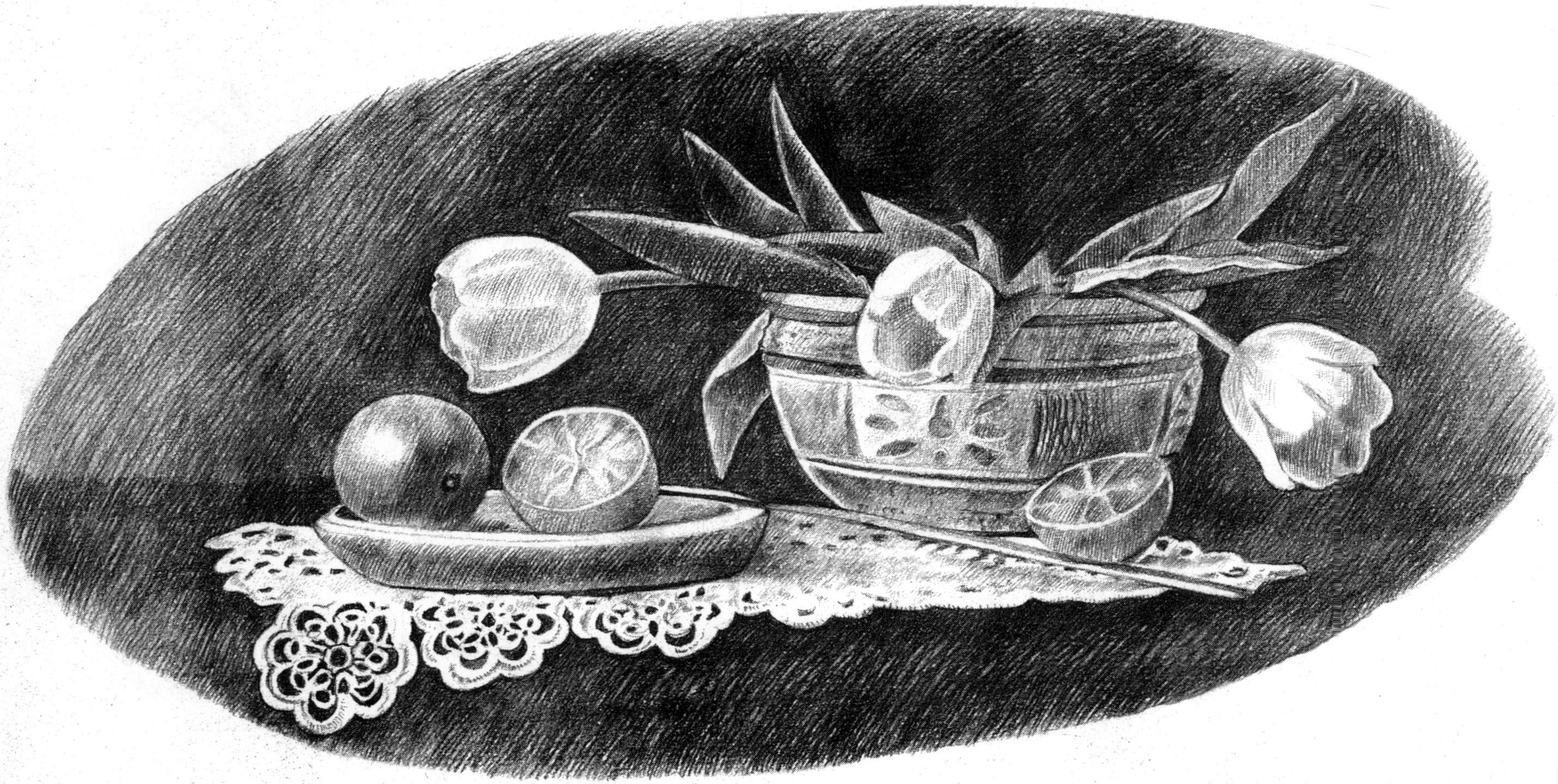

Observe the detailed contours of the lace.

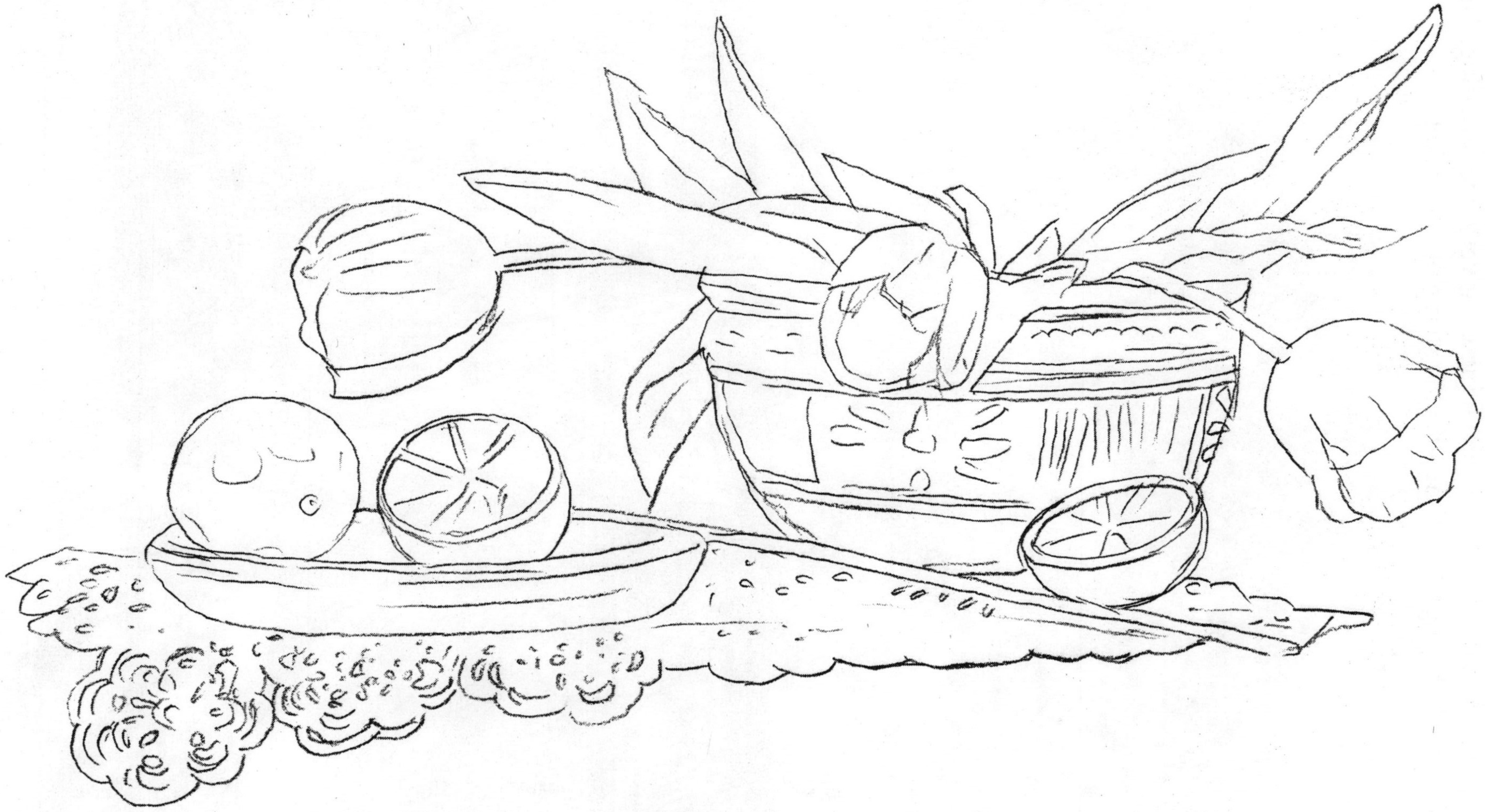

Observe the cut glass texture achieved by using very deep shading. The basket shading is done with hatching in rhythm with the shape of the basket.

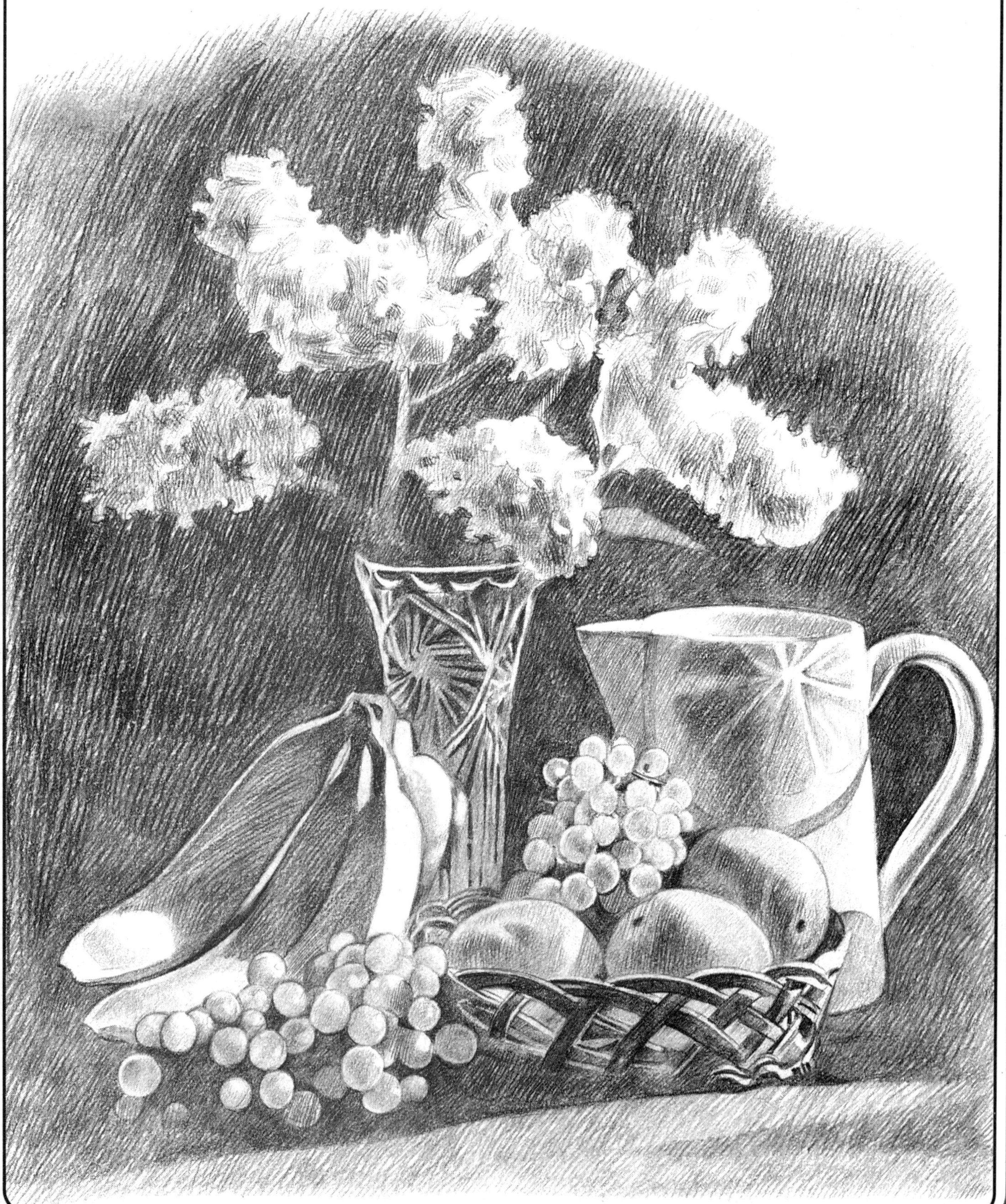

Draw the shapes of the object with strokes that follow the form.

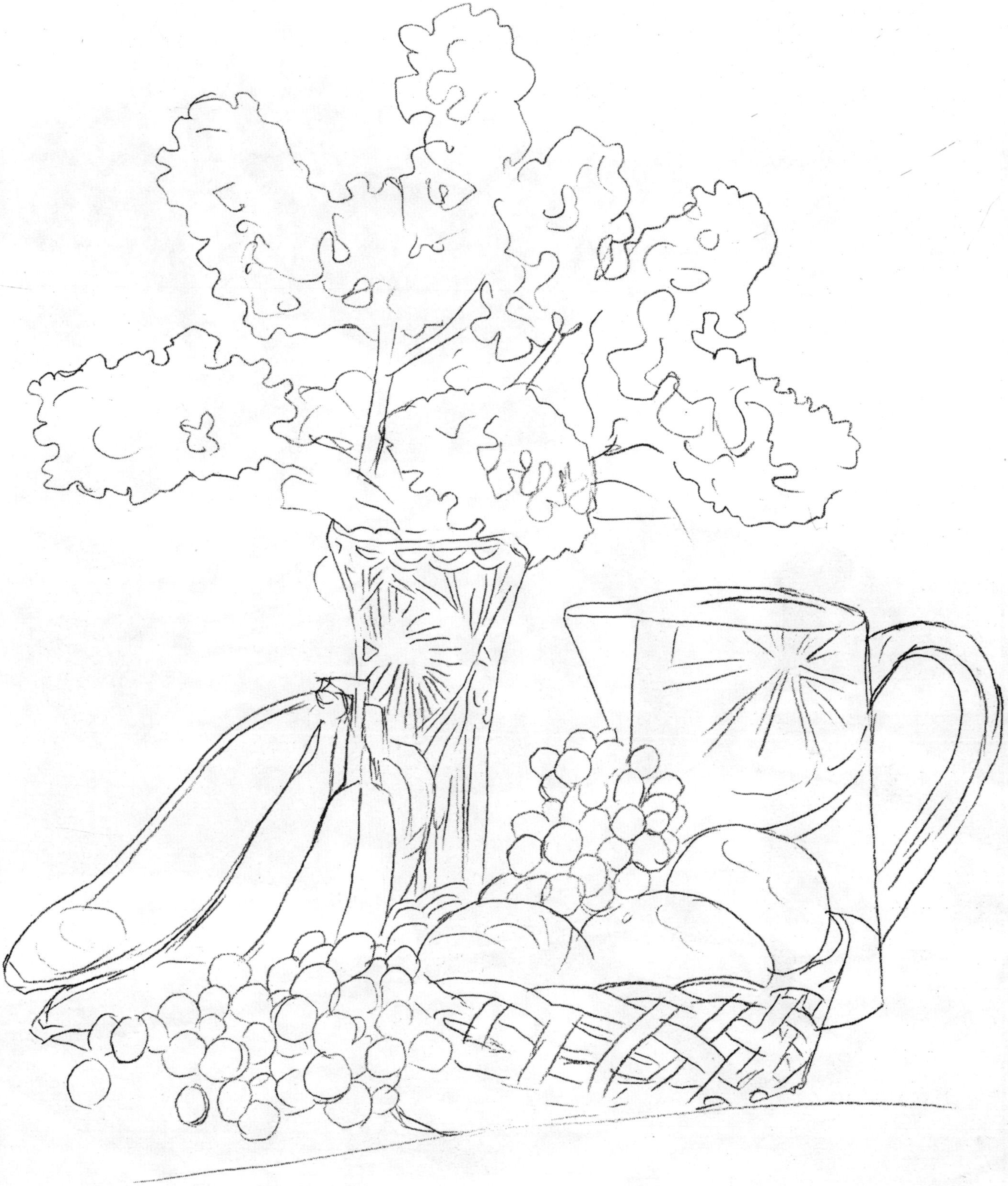

Render the capsicum to show its colour in different tonal values and shiny highlights, use pressure while drawing cross hatch for deep shades.

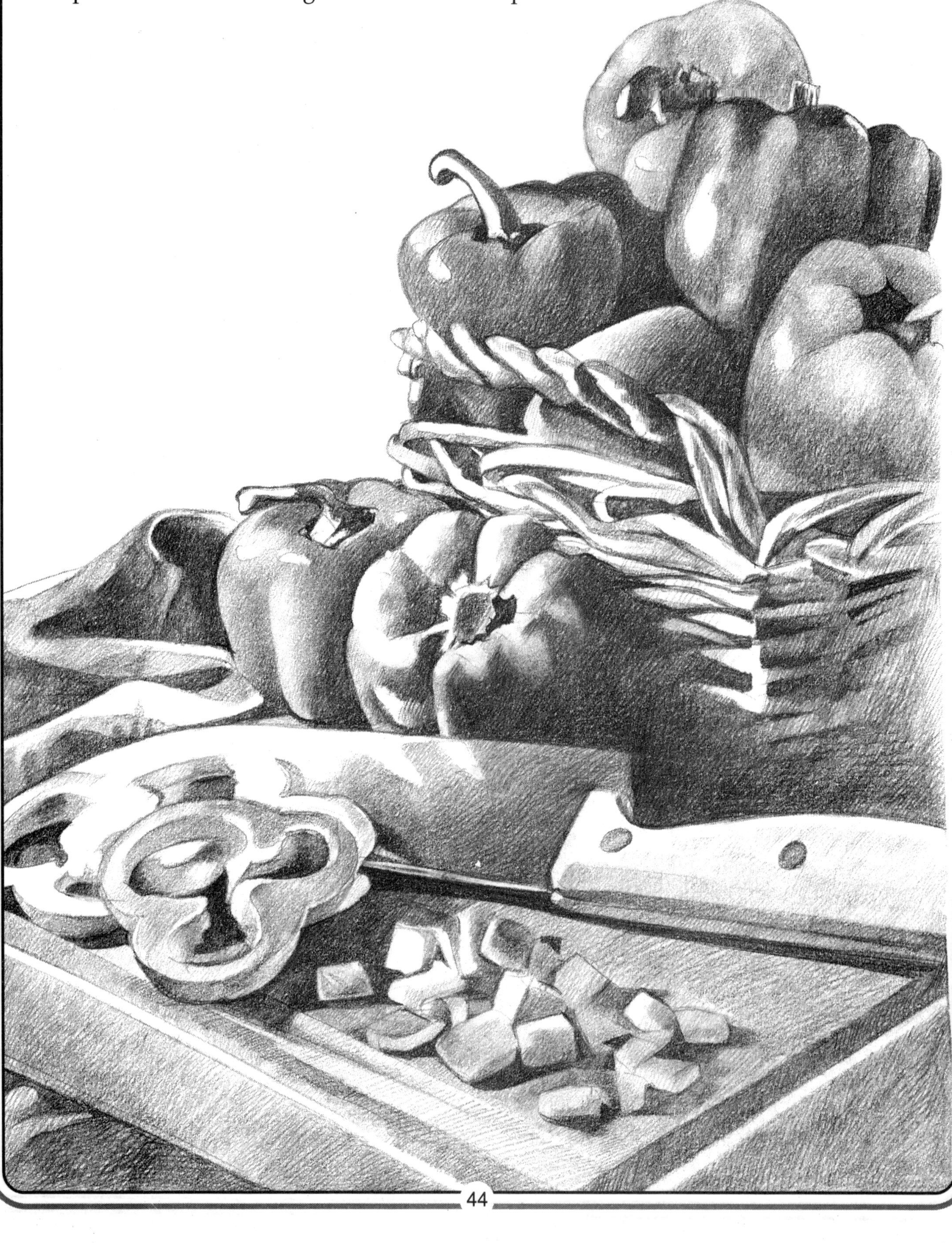

Concentrate more on the shape of objects, and reinforce your lines with sharp dark pencil where needed.

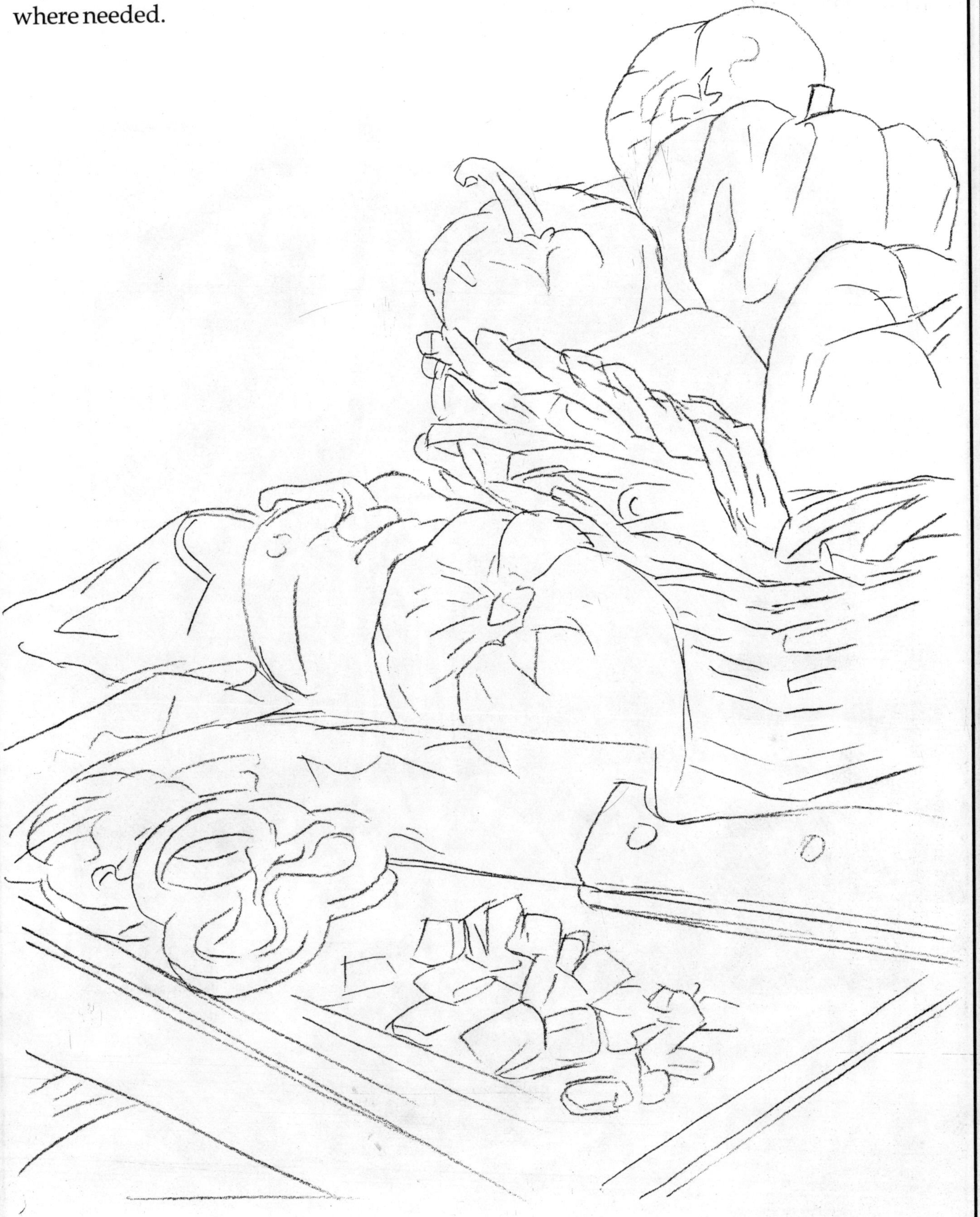

Render the deep colour of the flowers with strokes following the form to get the soft texture of the petals.

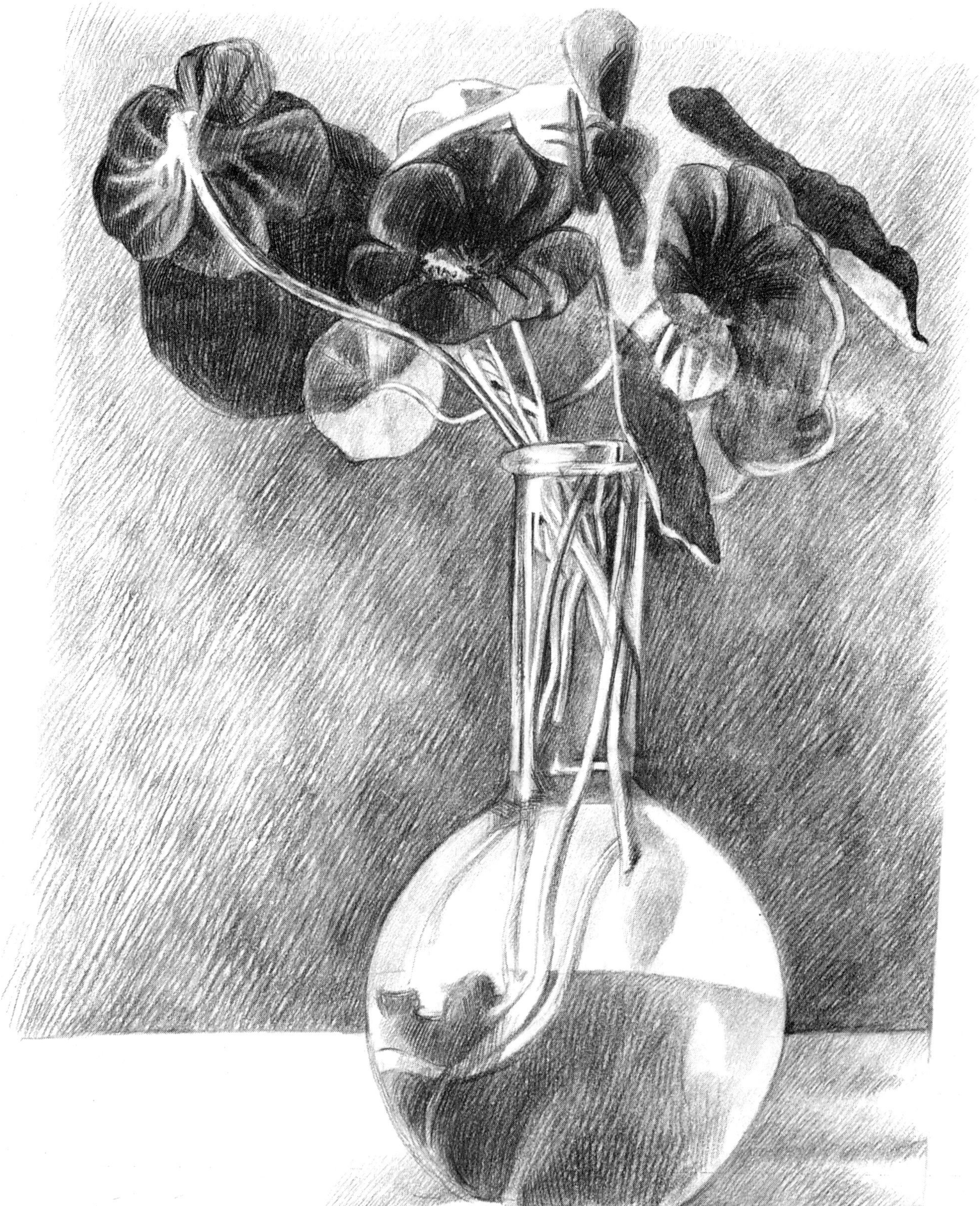

Study the curves of the petals, add details through multiple strokes while drawing the contour.

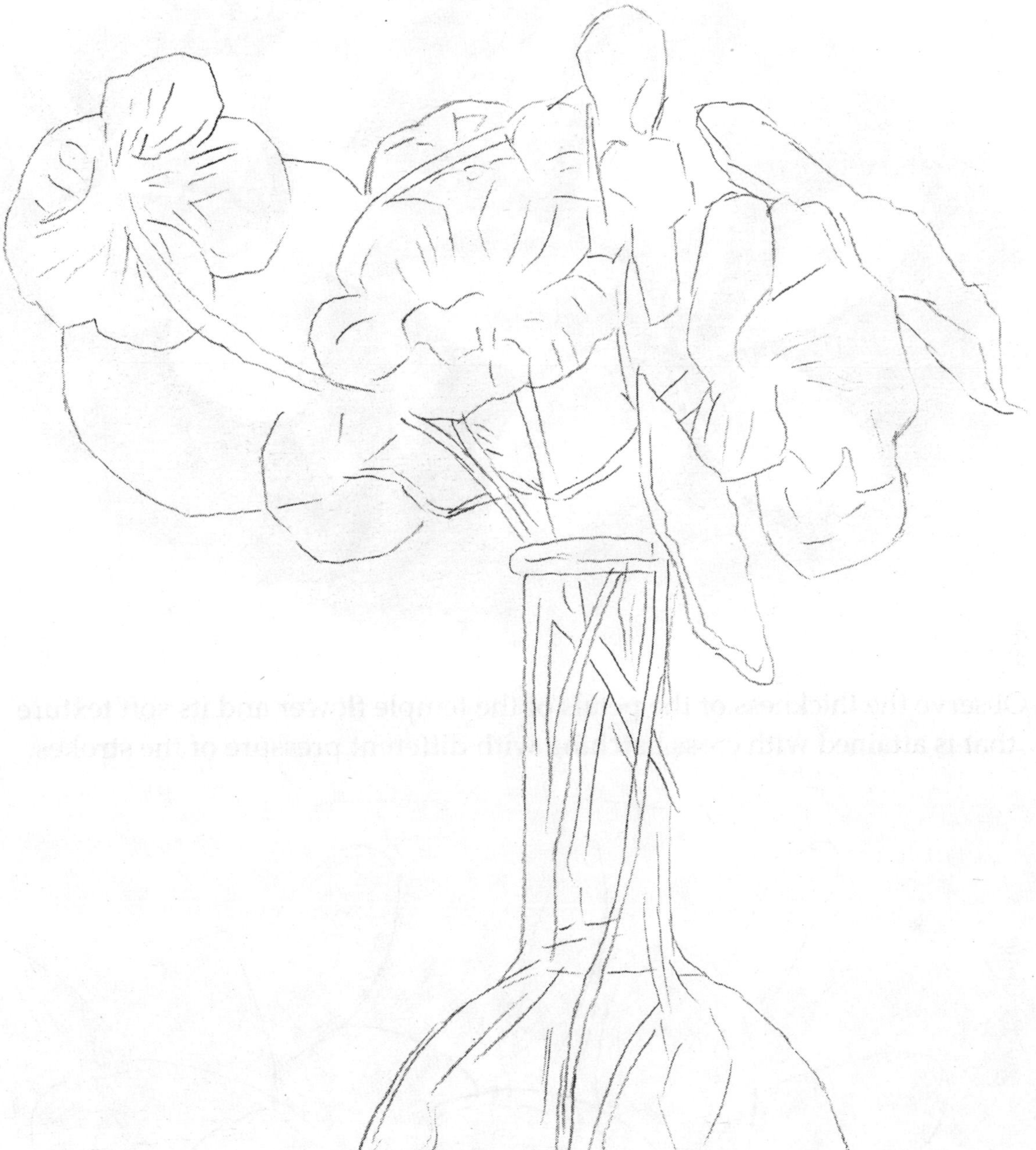

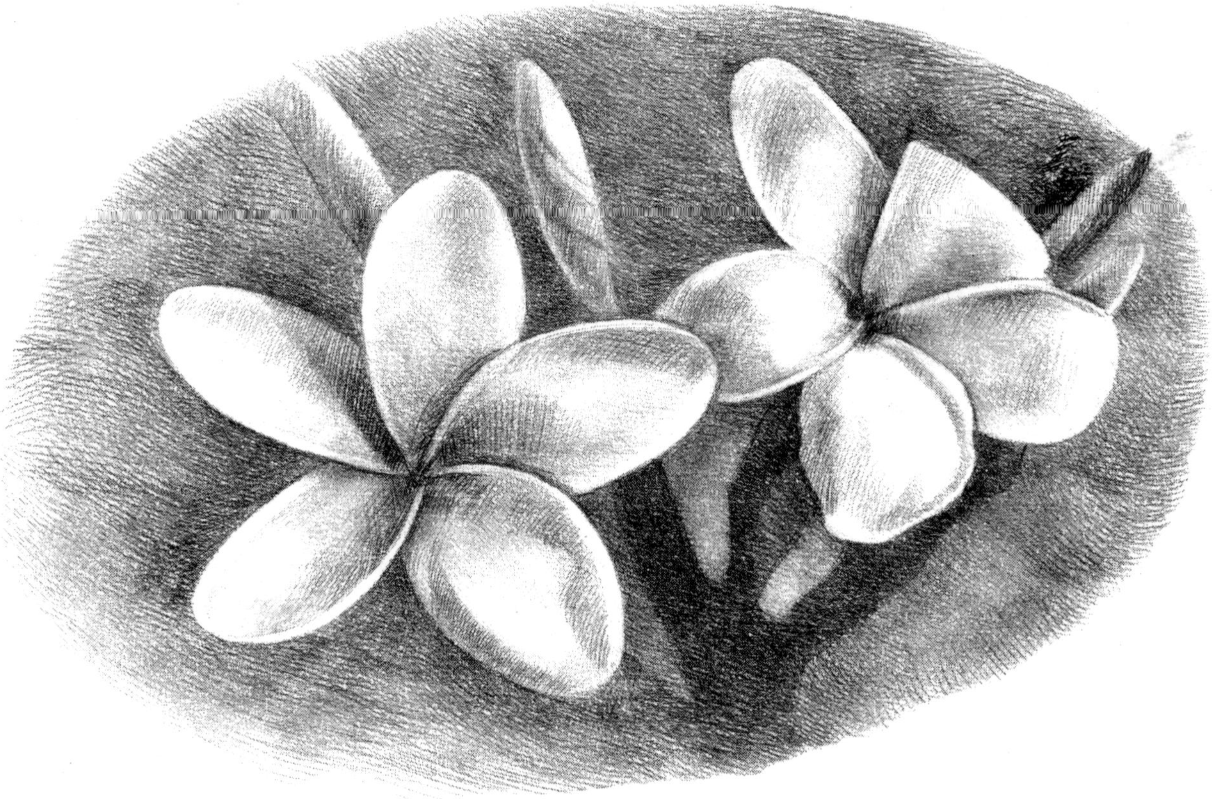

Observe the thickness of the petals of the temple flower and its soft texture that is attained with cross hatching with different pressure of the strokes.

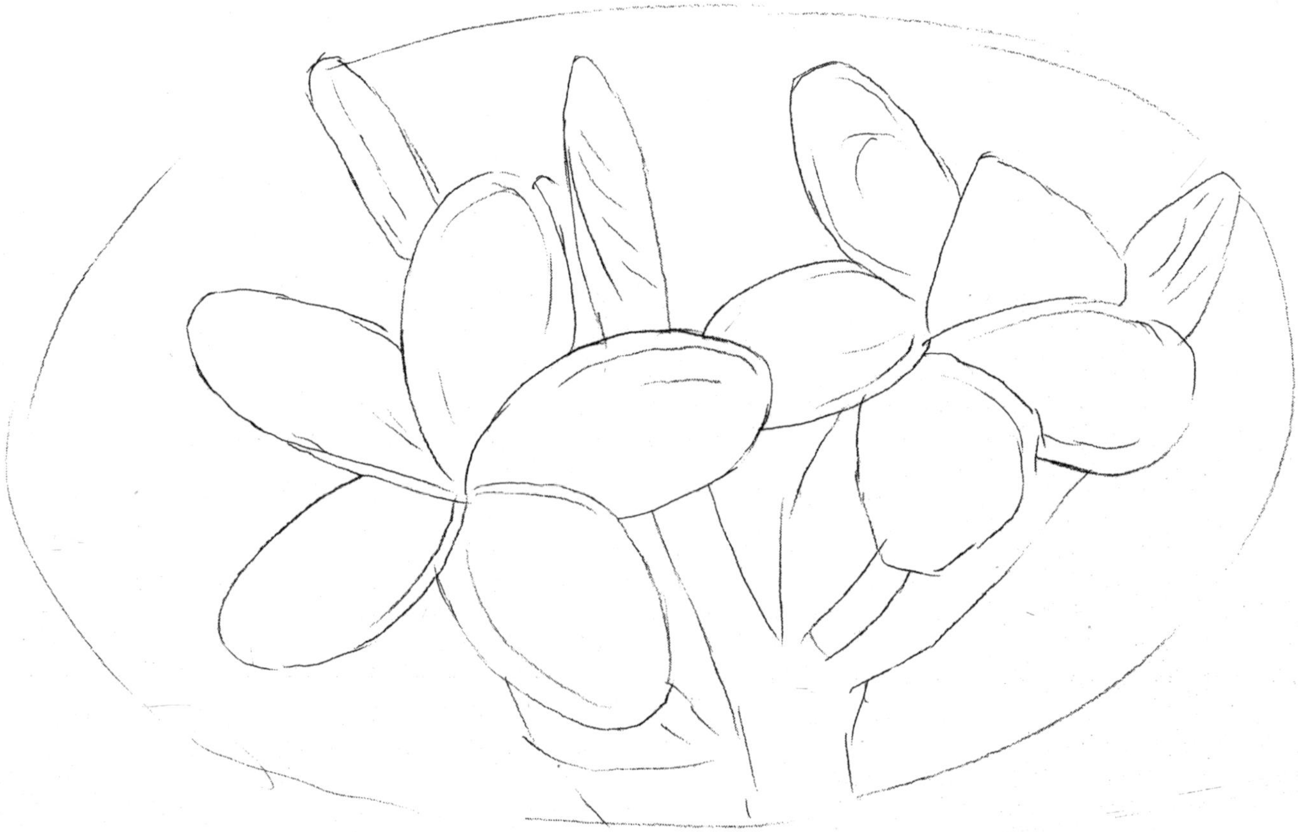